MW00776822

THE
EDUCATOR'S
HANDBOOK

THE
EDUCATOR'S
HANDBOOK

Principles, Reflections, Directives
of a Master Pedagogue
RABBI MORDECHAI I. HODAKOV

•

Compiled and arranged by
Rabbi Chaim M. Dayan
Rabbi Eli Friedman

•

Translated by
Yosef Cohen

Published by
MERKOS L'INYONEI CHINUCH
770 Eastern Parkway / Brooklyn, New York 11213

Copyright © 1998
by
Merkos L'inyonei Chinuch
770 Eastern Parkway / Brooklyn, New York 11213
(718) 774-4000 / FAX (718) 774-2718
e-mail merkos@chabad.org

Order Department:
291 Kingston Avenue/ Brooklyn, New York 11213
(718) 778-0226 / FAX (718) 778-4148
e-mail merkos@chabad.org

Library of Congress Cataloging-in-Publication Data
Hodakov, Hayim Mordekhai Ayzik, 1902-1993
[Hinukh veha-mehanekh. English]
The educator's handbook : a collection of directives
heard from Rabbi Mordechai I. Hodakov / compiled and arranged by
Chaim M. Dayan, Eli Friedman : translated by Yosef Cohen.
ISBN 0-8266-0688-1
1. Jewish religious education of children. 2. Habad.
3. Orthodox Judaism. I. Dayan, Hayim Me'ir.
II. Friedman, A. Eliyahu, haKohen. III. Title.
BM103.H2713   1998
296.6'8—dc21   98-20066
CIP

Printed in the United States of America

Rabbi Chaim Mordechai Isaac Hodakov

ז״ל

Latvian Ministry of Education Director Jewish Education;
Director Merkos L'Inyonei Chinuch, Machne Israel,
Agudas Chasidei Chabad;
Head of Secretariat of Lubavitcher Rebbe.

1902 –1993

TABLE OF CONTENTS

Analysis of Prayer / Affecting the Entire Day / Not to Pass in Front of Someone at Prayer / The Verse Corresponding to One's Name / The Chapter of Psalms Corresponding to one's Age / Prayer with a *Minyan* / The Sanctity of the Synagogue / Proper Behavior / Between *Minchah* and *Ma'ariv* / Explanations of the Prayers—A Sample Guide

COMPILER'S FOREWORD

Rabbi Chaim Mordechai Isaac Hodakov, late head of the secretariat of the Lubavitcher Rebbe, director of Machne Israel, Merkos L'Inyonei Chinuch and Kehot Publishing Society, and chairman of Agudas Chasidei Chabad—was an exceptional educator and pedagogue who is credited with many striking successes in the field of education.

Master pedagogue that he was, education was the central strand of his life and work and he threw himself into it with tremendous zeal throughout his long life. I was fortunate enough, as were many others, to receive first hand many words of advice and guidance in all aspects of education and child rearing, and Rabbi Hodakov further asked me to disseminate his words to educational institutions generally.

With G-d's help, I have managed to fulfill his wishes, and I present the book *The Educator's Handbook*, a collection of insights covering all aspects of education. The material for the book has been gleaned from the directives that Rabbi Hodakov issued both by phone and in writing to the principals of educational institutions in a variety of countries and at various periods. The factor common to them all is that they are without exception a beacon lighting the way to a fundamental Chasidic education in Torah and *yirat shamayim*, (fear of Heaven).

The material was edited and arranged by Rabbi Eli Friedman, emissary of the Rebbe to Safed, Israel.

This compilation is not an exhaustive one and anyone who has additional, hitherto unpublished material is requested to send it to us so that all may benefit from its inclusion, with G-d's help, in the next edition.

We are obliged to point out that this book derives, more than not, from the oral communications of Rabbi Hodakov as they were taken down by his listeners—but it was not presented to him for his final approval. It is our hope that we have conveyed his thoughts with the fidelity that is their due.

We have added source-references for Scriptural references and the sayings of our Sages. As concerns *halacha* (normative religious practice), our policy is to refer the reader to the *Kitzur Shulchan Aruch*, given the general familiarity with this work.

It is my pleasant duty to express here our gratitude and our esteem to all those who have helped and assisted us by passing along material for publication—particularly to Rabbi Nachman Sudak, director of Chabad-Lubavitch institutions in Great Britain, who was the channel for many of the directives issued by Rabbi Hodakov. We owe them all a great debt of thanks. May the blessing of their efforts rebound to them spiritually and materially.

Chaim Meir Dayan

Kfar Chabad, Israel
3 Shevat, 5755

TRANSLATOR'S INTRODUCTION

Rabbi Chaim Mordechai Isaac Hodakov was born in 1902 and passed away in 1993. In what was a long and energetically committed life, perhaps his overriding concern was for the spiritual and material welfare of all Jewish children—especially those with the least knowledge of Torah. One can imagine, for example, what his response might have been were he to have stumbled upon a segment of the young population seriously lagging in its social, economic and religious development: a flurry of phone-calls and memoranda, the 'grilling' of principals and administrators as to what steps were being taken to reach these dropouts, get them into beginners' yeshivas, contact their parents, find loving adult support for them if they were orphans, etc.

How clearly, as the following pages will show, did he understand the implications of such common terms as "can't keep up in school," "roam the streets," "have to belong to something"; and with what simple unshakable faith did he point to the teachings of the Torah as *the* antidote for this condition—Torah, and the proud traditions of the Chasidic movement in the whole-hearted attempt to save those deemed to be beyond repair.

He was a nuts-and-bolts man *and* a visionary and his uncompromising approach to standards—from punctuality to personal integrity—must have posed very serious problems for those of his associates who cherished notions of a private life, vacations and hobbies, self-cultivation, and the like. (Echoing the Rebbe, he argued that even one's desire to advance in spirituality had to be sacrificed to the need of the hour: the succor of Jewish souls crying out—even if themselves unaware of this—for guidance).

He was born in Beshenkevitch, Russia, at a time of great intellectual ferment in the Jewish world. He found his own vocation as an educator early on and his vision, of its scope and responsibilities reflected and was shaped by, the innumerable close contacts that he had, and was to have, with the sixth and seventh Lubavitcher Rebbes, Rabbi Yosef Yitzchak Schneersohn, of righteous memory, and his son-in-law, Rabbi Menachem Mendel Schneerson, of righteous memory.

This vision was energized and sustained by the stern stuff of his own nature. Indeed, he was a particularly Jewish embodiment of what is known these days as "tough love." This found its quintessential expression in what he demanded for, and of, the children in his charge.

He understood in all its implications the adage that the boy is father to the man. Where others saw in the child nothing more than unrestrained impulses, he saw latant buds of loving and responsible parenthood—the father taking his children to shul, molding their thoughts and feelings; the mother, nourishing the child's curiosity and aptitudes from the earliest age, creating an atmosphere from which its emotional life would never cease to draw strength.

The key, as he never wearied of saying, was "example." Bereft of this pivotal support, the Holy Writings themselves would remain words on a page, powerless to penetrate the child's mind and heart. The roles of teacher and parent—in his scheme practically interchangeable, so great is the influence he expects the teacher to exert—are paramount: the child comes to the love of G-d and the fear of G-d, and the attachment to His Torah, through what he absorbs from the adults around him. Woe to the child (woe to the adult!) who is only *told*, never *shown*.

To his students the teacher owes a total and selfless devotion. The dictum of the Sages: "The Torah views one who teaches Torah to the child of his fellow man *as if he had begotten him,*" Rabbi Hodakov interprets to mean: the teacher must take personal responsibility for the welfare of his charges, straddling the worlds of home and school in his efforts to remove obstacles to their growth and spiritual receptivity. And where the child is an orphan, or the product of a broken home, then truly no limits may be set to what the teacher must do by way of help, support and empathy.

The Educator's Handbook is a virtual *Kitzur Shulchan Aruch* of *Chinuch,* but beyond the 'standard' formulations of educational policy (many of which, like punctuality, table-manners and orderliness, are common to systems of every stripe, while many others: the proper way to pray; study methods in Mishna and Talmud; self-criticism, etc. typify the approach of many Jewish institutions) there is the specifically Chasidic dimension of the book, which has to do with the inculcation of joy, of *ahavat Yisrael,* and of all those attributes that go to make up the Chasidic personality. Herein lies the book's unique appeal.

More than knowledge or scholastic achievement, more than the ability to make a decent and an honest living, the author desires to impart an holistic vision enabling the child and the student to come to an appreciation of their place in the universe and of the mission they must fulfil if they are to achieve true happiness.

Within the framework of modern secular society, Rabbi Hodakov was a defender of the faith and of the soul. He saw, rather he registered with all his senses, the phenomenon that he dubbed "the atmosphere of the street," and took up arms against it, for he well understood its seductive and pernicious charms. The media, television in particular, were dominant elements of that atmosphere. He especially feared, because he understood, the influence of television on young minds the barrage of images against which they are defenseless (an observation confirmed, as it happens, by experimental psychology). Thus the mantra-like repetition, that what we see buries itself deep within the psyche and is able to rise to the surface, virus-like, even after being 'dormant' for many years.

He issued a plea: we must return to the simple and wholesome faith of our ancestors; we must recreate the atmosphere in which *they* lived, especially that of the weeks leading up to *Rosh HaShana* and *Yom Kippur*. And what made up this atmosphere if not the fear of Heaven, the awareness that one's deeds are recorded in a book; the aspiration to greatness in Torah; the readiness for sacrifice *al kiddush Hashem*.

He sought to place the means for the re-creation of this lost world within the reach of all: it began, quite simply, with the assertion, or the reassertion, of control over one's thoughts, one's eyes and one's tongue – as the Torah demands.

The reader will note that Rabbi Hodakov gave much thought to conditions in the Holy Land and much of the content of the Educator's Handbook revolves around the schools of the Lubavitch School Network in Israel, (*Reshet Oholei Yosef Yitzchak - Lubavitch*). Many of the children in these schools, perhaps a majority of them, were coming to Torah education and Torah life with little preparation in their youngest and most formative years. Not a small number were the products of broken homes, or were orphans. In fact, the chapter that most tellingly illustrates the author's compassion is precisely the one that deals with orphans. What is so striking here is his concern to have the needs of these children addressed, not only, or even primarily, in the institutional sense, but through the quality of personal involvement that their teachers and principals have with them—*as if they had begotten them*.

In other respects, Rabbi Hodakov was prepared to live with the times. In the spirit of the movement to which he devoted his life, always pressing ahead into the thick of things, he was not in the least squeamish about utilizing communications technology for *hafotzat haTorah* (the spreading of Torah) in the broadest sense. In a word, he was media-savvy, recognizing, for example, that film—if not its tawdry domain, the cinema—could make a positive contribution both to education and to the preservation of the educational experience.

His educational philosophy was a cradle-to-the-grave affair—in a word: Embrace them young, *raise* them, follow their progress when they leave, help and guide them, and be the first institution they turn to for their own children's needs!

The challenge of "the children of the street," is also the Jewish world's American challenge and its English challenge and its French challenge, etc., as assimilation and intermarriage – the final form this alienation takes - reach such proportions that the Rebbe himself has termed them "a spiritual Holocaust." It is our fervent hope that the thoughts of Rabbi Hodakov collected in this book will make their contribution to the "counter-revolution" that constitutes the return of the Jewish masses to their eternal source, the Torah.

•

A word on the translation. The raw material for the book, as explained by its compiler, Chaim Dayan, was taken down in note form, often from telephone conversations. Subsequently, there was no opportunity to submit the book to Rabbi Hodakov for polishing, emendation, and the like. Perhaps the principal challenge for the translator—more than the need to broaden and elaborate upon material that is at times of almost mishnaic brevity—has been to capture the voice of the man himself, his sometimes withering directness and *shtarkeit*, together with his tenderness, nostalgia and reverence for life.

That said, such force and fitness as the translation may possess could not have been achieved without the patient, rigorous and always perceptive editorship of Rabbi Yosef B. Friedman. His keen judgement has saved me from some stylistic excess as well as from sometimes misconstruing the author's intention. I take full responsibility for the shortcomings that remain.

Yosef Cohen

New York City, New York
Yud - Tes Kislev, 5759

CHAPTER 1

EDUCATION—TOP PRIORITY

THE VALUE OF EDUCATION

We must do our best to turn out students who will look to teaching, not simply as their livelihood, but as their *vocation*. Once the supreme importance and value of giving a Jewish child a Jewish education is explained, and put across with the necessary force, we will surely succeed in creating such an aspiration.

However, such an involvement must from the outset be motivated, not by concerns of *parnassah* (means of livelihood), but by a sense of the urgency of the undertaking, (*parnassah* is incidental, what counts is—the *chinuch*).

The *melamed* who is convinced of the centrality of education and aware of his particular responsibility, will not only strongly believe in what he is doing, (which is vital in any walk of life), but a sense of *special* responsibility will animate him, and this will explain the ardor, the zest and the *geshmak*—the relish—that he puts into, and gets out of, all his hard work.

CARING ABOUT EDUCATION

When working on some educational project, the idea must not be to hand out explanatory material and then think the job is done—surely there is more to it than that.

We must all be concerned about the negligence and lack of professionalism prevalent in the world of education today, even if we can do nothing about it—and how much more so if we can!

Things that Cause us Pain and Aggravation

When there is no milk for their children, parents will move heaven and earth to get it. And when a man is without an *etrog* (for Succot) he cannot give his mind to other things.

When one sees a house ablaze in the middle of the night, will he not rouse the occupants from their sleep and call out the fire brigade?—or will he just continue on his way as if it were none of his business!

When we suspect someone could be a terrorist or see a suspicious object, do we not have to do what we can to avert a catastrophe?

This is the outlook we must develop in the older students, so that when they see the state of education around them they will be shocked and feel impelled to intervene in order to do what they can to help.

Only the Qualified Need Apply

We should not be thought to be saying that someone who has no other means of livelihood should go ahead and try his hand at teaching! Quite the contrary: anyone who has the gifts and qualifications to become a *melamed*, will hopefully come to feel that this is his true, holy vocation, (and especially so in this day and age, when *chinuch* is an emergency rescue service); but let those who are not cut out for this look elsewhere for a livelihood!

Saving Souls

The educator must have the conviction that his work is vitally connected with the *soul*. The soul and the destiny of his young charges are in the hands of the educator, and a *chinuch* worthy of the name has as its proper sphere of activity the saving of souls. The foundation of the life of the Jew is the Torah, which charts a path for him through all the twists and turns and perplexing currents of life. The task of the educator is to teach the child how to live, and the destiny of the student depends upon the education he has received—it constitutes the grounds of his life and being, and this is entrusted to those responsible for his education!

TEACHING G-D'S CHILDREN

The Jewish people are called G-d's children. The teacher, the educator, is essentially the teacher of the child of G-d, the child of the King, and what more vital task can one perform? Thus it was that, starting with the Baal Shem Tov, the education of the Jewish child stood at the very forefront of the concerns of the leaders of Chabad-Lubavitch.

MELAMED VS. *SHLIACH*

Let all the young men committed to the cause of education have no doubts of the fact that the *melamed* is perhaps more important than the *shliach*. How so? The better part of a *shliach's* time is devoted to fund-raising, whereas the sole concern of the *melamed* is to disseminate Torah among his students! And what could better crown his labors than the fact that in his spare time the *melamed* is also engaged in *mivtzoim* (outreach activities of all kinds)—this graces his existence with a touch of true perfection, far beyond what the *shliach* can achieve!

THE LOFTY STATURE OF THE EDUCATOR

In his Talks, Rabbi Yosef Yitzchak Schneersohn of Lubavitch brings out fully the important stature of the *melamed;* indeed, many of the greatest chasidim were *melamdim.*

It is of course true that the lot of the *melamed* has not always been an enviable one, that he has not been looked-up to or well-recompensed. None of this was lost on the early chasidim, who nonetheless pressed on regardless, accomplishing whatever *chinuch* goals they had set out to accomplish.

THE LOVE OF ONE'S FELLOW JEW— A FUNDAMENTAL PRINCIPLE IN *CHINUCH.*

The vocation of the teacher is the quintessential expression of *ahavat Yisrael.* In fact, that this sentiment exists is the strongest argument for one's choosing to be a *melamed,* in order to have the possibility of bringing one's students closer to *Yiddishkeit.* Hence, *ahavat yisrael* is a fundamental principal in *chinuch.*

TO LEARN AND TO TEACH

We say in the blessing *"ahavat olam";* "and give us an understanding heart, to understand and to become wise, to listen, to learn and to teach."

We utilize the "eternal love" of G-d to request satisfaction of a multitude of needs—all with the ultimate purpose of "to teach"; but we fail to implement our own conclusions, our thoughts tend elsewhere and the "to teach" does not dominate our thoughts as it is supposed to do.

CHAPTER 2

THE PRINCIPAL— HIS RIGHTS AND DUTIES

THE ROLE OF THE PRINCIPAL

The role of the school principal is—to find out whether or not those working under him are carrying out in a proper and efficient manner, qualitatively and quantitatively, their tasks of *chinuch* and instruction, and to see to it that they are optimizing the time of the student and teaching at an appropriate level.

EXAMINING ONE'S CONSCIENCE

The principal must not allow himself to be satisfied with the number of students currently enrolled in his school; he must look beyond the current situation and work actively to boost the numbers. Each and every day he must ask of himself: what more do I have to do in order to have every child in town, or at least those living within the neighborhood of the school, become a student at my institution?

When on his travels he discovers a child who is not receiving a basic Jewish education, or a young man who has found himself a bride and built himself a house among the Jewish people, but not upon the foundations of Torah and *mitzvot*—then he must beat his breast and recite "*al cheit*" (words recited during *viduy*, confession), and not wait for *Yom Kippur*!

LIKE A FATHER

The school principal must always have at the back of his mind the statement of our Sages, (Rashi, *Bamidbar*, 3:1) "Whoever teaches his neighbor's son Torah is looked upon by the Torah as if he begot him." A father whose child is falling behind in school does everything he can to help him catch up, but without harsh words and embarrassing scenes. No less is expected of the principal.

THE SYLLABUS

Periodically, the syllabus should be reviewed, without relying upon the fact that it has "stood the test of time" and that "no one has problems with it." It may well be that until quite recently it achieved all that was expected of it, being well-suited to the capacities of the students. But now—times have changed, and the students are capable of greater things than was formerly the case.

This is of relevance to every institution and to every class.

CHARACTER

The personality and the character of the individual principal exercise a profound influence on the *melamed* and on his work with the students, and play an equally active part in the education of the child as well.

COMMITTEES OF REVIEW

A committee should be appointed, consisting of a number of individuals, (or of one person alone), whose task it is to look into the way the institution is run. To assess how things went in the past and how they are going in the present; the growth and the development of the institution; items in need of repair and improvement; how best to supplement what is already in place.

Once the year is under way, when the day-to-day demands of the institution take up so much time, it is difficult, if not impossible, to bring it to a standstill in order to carry out an in-depth study of its actual operation; and for the same reason it is difficult to make changes and improvements. However, the summer recess, when there is something of a break from the normal routines, is the ideal time for this. Then, at the commencement of the new semester, things will be on a surer footing, or will be more amenable to change during this period.

COMPLAINTS

In every institution there will inevitably be instances of teachers complaining about some aspect of the principal's way of running things. The perfect administrator has yet to be born— there *will* be complaints and there *will* be malfunctions in the system.

Accordingly, it is most important to allow grievances to be aired, so that the person concerned knows that his or her voice has been heard and that what he has to say has been noted in the proper quarters.

It is equally important to put him or her clearly in the picture. Sometimes differences will arise because the situation is not correctly understood. To the aggrieved party it can seem, therefore, that there is something seriously amiss, and if he is not disabused of this idea, it will buzz around in his head until he becomes convinced it is the truth—all because he was not given the courtesy of a response.

We find in fact that this is one of the forty-eight ways in which Torah is acquired—". . and give him a sure foundation in the truth." (*Avot*, 6:6) That is, it is our obligation to persuade others of the correctness and the truth of what we are doing, which leads to peace—". . . establish him in the ways of peace."

THE POTENTIAL WORTH OF EVERY PROPOSAL

Even a suggestion emanating from the most improbable source should not be dismissed out of hand—on the contrary, give it your serious attention. As is explained in *Hayom Yom* (9 Elul), even a simple person is capable of profound insights when the matter in question touches upon his vital interests.

STAFF MEETINGS

Any businessman worth his salt will from time to time take a close look at the way his business operates, with a view to changes and improvements that he may have to introduce if the business is to continue to prosper.

Similarly, doctors will convene periodically to exchange ideas on how standards of treatment might be improved.

The very same applies, but to an even greater extent, to the world of *chinuch*. The principal and his staff must meet from time to time in order to reach a consensus on the improvements, changes and additions that need to be made. Such a meeting is particularly important before the beginning of the new school year.

Keep in mind—whatever changes are made must be made to fit the present set of circumstances. It may well be that in former times things were done very differently, but the situation has changed, the reforms that are introduced must be able to "take" in the present set-up. It may be likened to the case of a man who appears at the factory gates looking for work, describing himself as a skilled laborer—just when the factory has become automated, and its work force replaced by machines!

There is a "covenant" with effort (to communicate essential truths)—that it will never be fruitless. When we take medicine, for example, the curative process begins instantly, with the taking of the first dose, even though we sense no change; and this is the case here—we must give the matter constant attention, the cumulative effect will be telling.

CHAPTER 3
DUTIES AND RESPONSIBILITIES OF THE EDUCATOR

A ROLE MODEL

An educator must remember at all times that he is a role model for his students. The conduct of the educator—vis-a-vis colleagues no less than students—has a profound influence on the development of the student's character, as well as on his day-to-day conduct. A great part of a student's education is shaped by this interaction with the educator; indeed, a child can pick up far more from even the most casual contact with its chief role model than from a semester's worth of lectures.

The teacher must recognize how much the education of the young depends upon his efforts, and how vital it is for him to set a consistent example in all that he says and does. Education must be a "living *Shulchan Aruch*." The educator must be scrupulous and precise in his approach to every single *halacha*. The student will register this and live with its influence for the rest of his life.

A THOROUGH KNOWLEDGE OF *HALACHA*

Educators at all levels must be thoroughly versed in the Laws of Talmud Torah (the learning and teaching of Torah), of *chinuch* and of *melamdim*, as expounded in the *Rambam* and in the *Shulchan Aruch*, and review them periodically. Let me illustrate the point in the following ways:

a. Every *shochet* (ritual slaughterer) must at intervals review the laws of *shechitah*, so that he be conversant in them and have them thoroughly memorized. (*Remo, Yoreh Deah*, beginning of Section 1).

b. Systematic study of the *halachot* of the Festival is begun thirty days before the date of the Yom Tov, and every year the process begins all over again, (*Pesachim*, 6a).

c. It is our practice to consult the *Shulchan Aruch* before embarking upon any significant undertaking, even when, in general, the *halacha* is known to us (see *Sefer haSichot*, 5704, p. 92).

d. There is a well-known story about the Rebbe, Rabbi Shalom DovBer of Lubavitch, who was once honored with *maftir*, but since he did not feel adequately prepared, the Rebbe went into a side room and reviewed the *Haftorah* privately, and only afterwards did he recite it before the congregation. This, in spite of the fact that he read this same portion every year.

Surely we should not be one iota less conscientious when it comes to the education of the Jewish child, this being a G-dly vocation! The teacher must understand, therefore, the extent to which the *Shulchan Aruch*, with all its weight of authority, holds him responsible for the proper performance of his task.

Every time we study, new aspects of the subject are revealed to us, whose existence we did not even guess at until now.

ASPIRING TO HIGHER THINGS IN *CHINUCH*

Every teacher should aspire to go higher and further in *chinuch*. That he has such an ambition gives vitality to his pedagogic labors; absent this, all becomes stale and listless. From time to time the *melamdim* should take a critical look at the level of education that they are providing to the students, putting their heads together in order to devise ways to improve and perfect—never resting content with the status quo.

An educator or teacher who is an expert in his field, particularly one with years of experience, is now in a stronger position than ever before to influence and benefit his student. He must, however, be fully cognizant of this if he is to make use of this extra potential.

SELF-PERFECTION

There is always room, not simply for improvement, but for one quantum leap after another. Indeed, this must become an end in itself: to reach for the ultimate in perfection.

Take the average workman, whose handiwork may be riddled with imperfections; and the master craftsman, whose handiwork is capable of reaching perfection of beauty and form. How do we account for the contrast? The answer lies in the fact that the latter has mastered his craft, and that night and day his thoughts return to the same question: how can I reach an even higher level of mastery?

Similarly, you have the teacher who does his job conscientiously and makes good use of his time; but he is not a master of the craft of teaching—this individual must work harder to perfect his craft, by seeking out experts in the field, watching them in action and assimilating all he can. Which is not to say that even the finest craftsman cannot reach a higher level—the only limits are those one sets for oneself!

TEACHERS CONVERSING

The relationship between the teacher and his colleagues, even outside the walls of the classroom, should be mutually dignified and respectful. In fact, because students are so impressionable, this relationship may actually affect the quality of their education. The same is true of the teacher's relationship with the director and principal.

Teachers must go to great lengths to ensure that their conversation be dignified, especially in front of their students. And how much more must they be careful not to slight another teacher in front of the student.

Sometimes, the contrary takes place—a teacher addresses a colleague by his first name in an offhand manner; indeed, because he fails to strike the right note of formality, his manner of speaking sounds more like banter. The student exposed to this receives a negative impression. And he cannot be expected to know that he is standing before old friends who perhaps were *chavrusas*—study partners—in yeshiva! All that *he* sees is that adults whom he looks up to, and who occupy positions of responsibility, are capable of conversing in this way.

In the years immediately following the arrival in the United States of Rabbi Yosef Yitzchak of Lubavitch, the room that now serves as the office of the Merkos L'inyonei Chinuch served as a classroom. The Rebbe's room was on the second floor, above this one. I was once there when the Rebbe heard one of the teachers addressing his colleague by his first name, without a formal title, in front of the students. The Rebbe told me that we must deal with this lapse at once in order to prevent any repetition of such behavior. Granted that when chasidim speak among themselves they dispense with formalities—nevertheless, in front of the students they should refrain from doing so. This is particularly the case where a student might be exposed to an ugly scene between a teacher and his colleague, at which time a most unfortunate impression would be made upon him.

SETTING GOALS

The educator must know from the outset what to expect of the student. He has to set a target for himself, and when this target is attained he has to set another.

Just as nobody should let a day go by without exerting himself to reach a higher level, (so much so that in the words of our Sages [*Tana D'vei Eliyahu Rabba*, Ch. 28] everyone must say, "When will my deeds resemble those of my forefathers, Avraham, Yitzchak and Yaakov?"), so should he strive to bring the student to a higher level.

DOCTOR OF THE SOUL

The duty of the teacher is to know what to study with the students and how to study it. Just as a doctor must give appropriate and precise medication to the patient, so too must the *melamed*, the "doctor of the soul," give the student the spiritual cure—*chinuch*—appropriate to his case, and in the right "dosage." Otherwise, he betrays his trust, Heaven forbid, and is no better than a doctor who prescribes the wrong medication.

The teacher must be thinking constantly about the student—what to teach him, how to teach him, and all in accordance with the capacity of the student.

CHINUCH—A FORCE FOR CHANGE

Chinuch must penetrate to the innermost parts of the person, to the springs of action. The mere imparting and receiving of knowledge are not enough—rather, the material absorbed must manifest itself in practical terms, in thought, speech and action.

The educator must aim to produce truth-seekers, men of action.

EVERY CHILD'S POTENTIAL FOR GREATNESS

We have to regard every child the way we would regard one of the great figures in our history. Even Moshe Rabbeinu was a Jewish child, with all the limitations of a child—only in the fullness of time does he become Moshe Rabbeinu!

All is in the hands of the educator!

CONSOLIDATION THROUGH REPETITION

A teacher who has covered a topic with his students on one or two occasions—must review the topic after a certain period of time. There are several reasons for this.

First, it is quite possible that little of it was retained. Second, the students may not have paid adequate attention the first time round and missed important points.

Third, the students are further along now; consequently, their "take" on things has changed, and the topic may be presented in a more mature and challenging manner!

Fourth, it is next to certain that they will now be able to make sense of some novel insight that they could not grasp previously. All the more so on account of the fact that this is *limud ha-Torah*, where from year to year we enter more deeply into the topics that were presented to us, even originating insights of our own.

Fifth, it is probable that in the interim new students have been added to the class.

ALWAYS ON DUTY

The educator must be "on the job" twenty-four hours a day, seven days a week, three hundred and sixty five days a year. He who teaches the child of his friend Torah is looked upon as if he had begotten him, and just as the love of a mother for her child never takes a vacation, so also is it forbidden to permit any gaps to open up in the work of the educator.

TRUANCY

When a child skips class—the educator must inquire into his whereabouts and activities during that time, and he is not to assume that all is well simply because the parents have given permission for the child to be absent.

PARENTS AND TEACHERS

Were we to give thought even for a moment to the care and attention that parents lavish on their children, we would grasp something of the immense privilege and responsibility that are the portion of those who teach their fellow-man's child Torah.

Parents pray that their children may be sound in wind and limb. In the eyes of the parent a healthy child is one who acts, and develops, normally. Similarly, one meal a day is certainly not considered adequate, and the parent will also take pains to provide the child food prepared in an appetizing manner.

So it is that when parents deliver their children to the school, they expect that they will be provided with a complete and comprehensive program and, by the same token, that their personalities will be developed in a full and well-rounded manner.

THE TEACHER AS CARETAKER

The teacher's task is similar to that of a caretaker, (the halachically-defined functions performed by one whom the Torah designates as such). The responsibility of the caretaker for the article entrusted to him runs without interruption from the moment that he takes it into his safekeeping until he returns it to the owner. And if he lets the article out of his sight even for a moment and it is stolen, he is automatically guilty of negligence and must pay compensation. So it is here: the child who is sent for an education is the educator's responsibility for the entire time, without interruption. Every educator must take note of this and be fully aware of its implications.

THE REBBE'S INTEREST IN EACH AND EVERY STUDENT

The Rebbe, Rabbi Yosef Yitzchak of Lubavitch relates in one of his talks (*Sefer Ha-Sichot*, 5705/1945, p. 44) that in the year 5672-1912, he came to see his father, Rabbi Shalom DovBer, in Menton, and although the Rebbe desired to be brought up to date in all communal matters, the very first question he had for his son concerned the well-being of each and every student in the Yeshiva Tomchei T'mimim. Nor was he interested in hearing generalities, but insisted upon being given a detailed account.

Here, too, we learn the overriding importance of keeping the welfare of each and every student uppermost in one's mind at all times.

CHAPTER 4
THE TEACHER-PUPIL
RELATIONSHIP

"I'M BUSY RIGHT NOW"

It happens, more often than one would like, that a student asks or requests something of the teacher or the Principal, only to be told: "I'm busy right now." This kind of response has a most unfortunate effect on the student.

In Riga once, I was present in the synagogue at a time when Rabbi Mordechai Dubin was giving a class in Talmud. Someone came up and put some questions to him. Showing not the least sign of impatience, he took his time to listen to the man, answering him with a smile, cordially, in spite of the fact that his time was hardly his own, (he was also at the time a member of the Latvian House of Representatives).

AUTHORITY

A key factor in education is the authority the teacher should ideally have vis-a-vis the student. Without this authority, the word "influence" is robbed of all meaning. Indeed, nothing must be allowed to impair this authority, since it takes relatively little to block the student's receptivity to things that we wish to instill in him.

The *Mishnah* (*Avot*, 4:12) says: "Let the fear of your teacher be like your fear of Heaven." The reason for this is that the teacher is a link in the chain that goes back to Moshe Rabbeinu, who received the Torah of Hashem at Sinai. The student must understand and must feel that the teacher is not making any innovations of his own, but that he is the continuation of the tradition that began with Moshe Rabbeinu, through whose voice the *Shechina* itself (the Divine Presence) spoke.

CONNECTING

The student must have the feel that the educator takes a genuinely personal interest in him. Even when he finds it necessary to rebuke or punish him, it has to be done in the manner of "the left rebuffs and the right draws near"—with firmness and with love.

THE HONOR OF THE STUDENT

"Let your student's honor be as dear to you as your own," (*Avot*, 4:12). The choice of words here is critical—"dear," not "sensitive," or the like. An educator must be sensitive to the "lovable" element that is latent within the honor of the student, be it in the general sense—a young child is an innocent in whom there is not the stain of sin—be it in the particular—every student possesses the most precious qualities. "As your own"—one's attitude to the student should be very much like a person's attitude towards himself: he is exquisitely attuned to all that concerns him, is jealous of his honor, and desires that his fellow men honor him.

AS IF HE HAD BEGOTTEN HIM

All educators should take to heart the words of our Sages (Rashi, *Bamidbar*, 3:1) that "One who teaches Torah to the child of his neighbor is regarded by the Torah as if he had begotten him." We take this to mean that in a very real sense the educator has himself brought into the world the child that sits before him, that the child whom he is educating is *his child*. Such a conception certainly helps establish a strong and loving connection between student and teacher.

To my mind, however, the statement is to be explained in the following way: at the very moment that one decides to "teach his neighbor's son Torah" it is already "as if he himself brought that child into the world."

ATTENDING TO THE PHYSICAL AND THE SPIRITUAL

It is the duty of the educator to concern himself with the welfare of every student as if he or she were his own flesh and blood; just as he turns to his own child—out of love and devotion showing fatherly concern and tenderness—so should his feelings be vis-a-vis his own students. And "just as on the surface of the water face reflects face," so will the student return his love, and love the school where he receives his education.

When the teacher sees that a student has not handed in his homework, or is showing signs of fatigue, he should have a word with him in private and find out whatever he can: does he get enough sleep? what is his family situation? Beyond this, he should arrange to visit his home, to see how the parents are getting by, and whether they enjoy a reasonable standard of living.

If a student come to school in torn, shabby clothing, this fact should alert the teacher to the possibility that the parents are in need of assistance. To help lift the student's spirits, Yom Tov clothing should be purchased for him, (see *Kitzur Shulchan Aruch*, ch. 103:5), but in a way that does not cause him embarrassment.

Every student should be treated in this way, in the sense that the school shows sensitivity to his or her particular needs, physical and spiritual, and does what it can to address them.

Watching our Tongues

It has been known to happen that, at recess, when teachers enter the staff-room, one of them will be relating some amusing incident involving one or another of his students, and another student will chance to be in the room just at that moment, only to overhear the teacher making merry at a fellow-student's expense. This can have very serious repercussions.

First, the teacher has broken the prohibition not to indulge in idle gossip.

Second, in educational terms, the student could not be set a more distasteful example.

Third, he will go straight to his friend and reveal to him that he was the butt of the teacher's jokes, with the result that the affair will eventually reach the ears of the boy's parents.

Fourth, the following year this boy may find himself in a class taught by this teacher, in which case it is not difficult to imagine the level of respect he will feel towards that teacher.

The Previous Year's Reports

Every teacher receives his class reports from the colleague who taught that class the previous year, and he sets to work on the basis of these reports. This approach is a mistaken one, since it may well be the case that in the interim the weak student has raised his standards and the miscreant, mended his ways.

This is a point no educator can afford to lose sight of.

CHAPTER 5
SCHOOL, CLASSROOM, DORMITORY

THE BEGINNING OF THE SCHOOL YEAR

Commencement should take place before 18th Elul, at the latest. Better still, wherever possible things should get underway even before this date. By such an arrangement, not only do we spare the children a certain amount of enforced idleness, but they gain in the most obvious manner—they learn more, hear the blowing of the shofar, and so on.

THE FIRST DAY OF STUDIES

Studies on the first day should begin in a festive mood, with an assembly in order to hear stirring and inspirational speeches, all of which should help to ensure that the year gets off to a rousing start.

YALKUT YOMI

I would find it gratifying to hear that use was being made of the booklet "Yalkut Yomi," and that one or more pieces selected from it were being taught daily, or weekly. It contains didactic material of great value.

THE SCHOOL AND ITS UPKEEP

Particular importance should be given to the upkeep of the school and its decor, as an attractive school building promotes a sense of well-being in students and visitors alike. The eyes of the student arriving at school should light upon a clean and well-maintained institution, classrooms as well as grounds. The fact that there are well-tended lawns and flower-beds will give delight. In the same way, everything else relating to the physical appearance of the school should be pleasing to the eye, since this is also implied in the words "This is my G-d and I will adorn Him," (*Beshalach* 15:2, *Shabbat*, 133b). Such things endear the school to the student, and especially so when he or she comes from a home which is without aesthetic appeal. It will also, I believe, have a "ripple effect," through the agency of students who have siblings in other institutions, as these will envy them the charm and splendor of their school, and over time they too will be brought into the orbit of a Jewish education.

Neatness and tidiness in the classroom lay a foundation for order and discipline. When, on the other hand, a student has to function in the midst of clutter and mess, he or she will become slipshod and negligent in all areas, including behavior.

THE WELL-APPOINTED CLASSROOM

The administration should see to it that classrooms are decorated with posters and suitable verses from Scripture. There are two reasons for this:

First, we create a pleasant and a cultured environment, in which the student's appetite for knowledge is progressively stimulated and gratified, stimulated and gratified.

Second, everything that a child sees becomes engraved in its mind, (and this is the reason for our putting up pictures of the

Rebbeim—so that a prominent place in its mental world should be occupied by the image of the *tzaddik*.) By giving preference to decoration of this sort we enhance the prospects of such material making a deep and permanent impression on the child's mind.

THE BINDING OF BOOKS

We must not neglect to cover text-books and *seforim*.

GIVING CHARITY DAILY

Every child should give charity daily, and a double amount on *erev* Shabbat—to include Shabbat, (on which the handling of money is forbidden). Children should get into the habit of giving *tzedaka* even on days when school is suspended, as well as during vacations.

LUNCH-TIMES

During lunch-times, *nigunim* should be played over the public address system, alternating with simple *halachot* or brief sayings taken from *Hayom Yom*—which will help to instill good manners and civility.

"AL NAHAROT BAVEL," "AVAR'CHA"

Teachers should make sure that the students recite the various psalms before *Birchat Hamazon*. We fully expect them to know the meaning of these verses, too.

MAYIM ACHARONIM

Always see to it that the children wash *mayim acharonim.* This practice seems to have "gone out of fashion."

Parenthetically, even at weddings and other celebrations, one finds that *mayim acharonim* is not brought out for the participants at the end of the meal.

BIRCHAT HAZIMUN*

We must not allow the students to neglect to recite this section of the *"bentching."*

RECESS

Recess should be used constructively, *and* for keeping an eye on the students while they are at play. This is an additional feature of our efforts to help them make the most of their time.

During recess the teacher should observe the students most attentively. Sometimes, words of love and concern, spoken while the children are at play, can in the blinking of an eye forge a lasting bond between teacher and student.

THE PHOTOGRAPHING AND FILMING OF EVENTS

Every school event of a festive nature should be captured on film. This serves a twofold purpose. First, there will be a permanent record of the history of the school. Second, the filming of the event is a clear indication of its importance and will help the students better to appreciate this fact.

---

* The responsive phrases recited before the Grace After Meals.

WELCOMING GUESTS

When a "new face" arrives in town, someone, let us say, with the stature of one of the Rebbe's emissaries, all the children should be assembled, so that the guest can be presented to them. Such visits are likely to leave a lasting impression.

HOMEWORK

When a student fails to hand in his homework, the real culprit may be the fact that he had no supper the previous evening—find out if this is the case. Other symptoms may be present—the child could be restless or nervous, the whole day long, but from essentially the same causes.

THE GOOD COMPANION QUESTIONNAIRE

Every day in the morning blessings we say, "and preserve me today and every day . . . from an evil companion." We must show how important it is to have a good companion, and explain what it is that distinguishes the good companion from the evil one.

I once asked a principal point-blank: "What *is* a good companion?" He could not answer me!

Some of our institutions devise a questionnaire for their students, containing such questions as: What is a good companion? What is an evil companion? together with other simple and direct questions of this type. From the answers of the students it was possible to get an idea of their general attitude toward this subject. Subsequently, we were able to go into things more deeply with them and to bring about some desirable changes in the sphere of human relations. In my opinion, questionnaires along these lines should be used in every educational institution.

PERSONAL QUESTIONNAIRE

Every student should be given a personal questionnaire to complete, something that will help the educator discover where he "stands" in relation to Torah and *mitzvot*. Does he, for example, wear a *talit katan* the entire day or only part of it? etc...

ADVISABILITY OF MAINTAINING A CARD INDEX FILE

Just as every medical practitioner maintains a file for each and every one of his patients, educators should maintain files for their students. Entries should include: family and economic situation, domestic conditions, mode(s) of transport to and from school, days of absence, free time in which there is more opportunity for backsliding than for spiritual growth, (*Shabbat* and festivals, for example) and, of course, something on the character of the student.

LEARNING BY HEART

The children should be encouraged to learn by heart various sections in *Chumash* and *TaNach*, (such as *Az yashir*, *mishnayot*, *Pirkei Avot*, sayings of *Chazal*, *halachot*, and so on).

This applies across all age groups and academic levels.

When words of Torah are engraved upon the mind, there need never be a moment when its holy letters are not before the mind's eye, allowing us to concentrate all our thoughts on them. Similarly, the beneficial effects will flow beyond the boundaries of self, for the atmosphere of a house permeated with the letters of Torah is of an altogether different order of purity, a phenomenon which is explained in *Hayom Yom* (4 Cheshvan), and the beneficial influence of the letters becomes embodied in the decisions taken in the home.

BIRTHDAYS

When a birthday arrives the teacher should wish the student a hearty *mazal tov!*—this can do their relationship nothing but good. In addition, he should send a letter of blessing to the parents, and wish them *mazal tov* too.

The study period may be somewhat shortened to make room for a birthday-party. This can be beneficial in several ways: it helps to strengthen brotherly feelings among the students; the youngster will never forget the positive experiences he has had at the school; it will lead to more cordial relations between parent and teacher.

At the party the teacher should explain the customs connected with birthdays, and something should be said about the chapter of *Tehillim* corresponding to the age of the birthday boy, or girl.

Be aware of the fact that before the secular birthday can be converted into its Hebrew equivalent, we have to know at what hour the boy or girl was born—before sundown or after—given that in the secular system one counts from midnight, whereas in the Jewish calendar one counts from sundown.

MONTHLY JOURNALS

Every month, a modest-sized journal or magazine should be distributed, from which, week by week, the children will learn practical *mitzvot* and be engaged by material that highlights conduct. All this will be based on the weekly *parsha*, in a way that will help the children "live with the times," that is, with the *parsha* of the week.

There should also be a special section in the journal which describes the ways to acquire good character traits, such as civility, respect for social conventions, table manners, the obligation to avoid causing others distress, to lend a helping hand, as with loading and unloading; and with the removal of undesirable traits, such as anger, pride, vengefulness and the bearing of grudges.

CHANUKAH AND PURIM PARTIES

Parties should be organized in honor of Chanukah and Purim, providing the opportunity for the children to perform before their parents.

CHABAD HOUSE

The closet of every student in the dormitory is his own "Chabad House." In it he should keep: a *Siddur*, in which should be written (inside the front cover, the words of the psalm:) "The earth is the L-rd's and its bounteousness," together with his full name; a box for *tzedaka* (not left until it is full, to discourage theft); and a *Chumash*. In this way the closet will remind its owner of the purpose of life, and he will be mindful of the three pillars of the world: Torah (*Chumash*), Divine service (*Siddur*), and the performing of good deeds (the *tzedaka* box).

A SOUVENIR FOR THE GRADUATE

Graduating students should be presented with a photograph of the school. This photograph will accompany them on their life's journey, a memento of all the positive and enriching things that they experienced during their time at school.

CHAPTER 6

THE CLASSROOM—
MAKING EVERY MOMENT COUNT

HOW TO CAPITALIZE ON CLASS TIME

Making full use of every minute spent in school and infect-ing students with the same "virus"—this is one definition of the successful teacher. The students in turn must be fully aware that the teacher treasures every moment and tries to extract every ounce of worth from it. This will call forth in them a determi-nation themselves to measure up to the teacher's level of com-mitment.

By the same token, if the student sees that the teacher does not make proper use of class time—that he or she does not ar-rive punctually, is not well organized, does not maintain stan-dards, etc.—he will understandably end up thinking to himself: why should *I* be so conscientious? In the process he will develop a lackadaisical attitude towards school work and the time spent in school will come to mean less and less to him.

EVERY MINUTE DOUBLED

The teacher who is unpunctual becomes responsible for wasting the time of every student in the class—and this increases exponentially, according to the number of students present! And as if this were not enough, halachically he is regarded as one "who does G-d's work in a fraudulent manner," as explained in the *Shulchan Aruch* (*Kitzur*, 165:12).

LATENESS AFFECTS DISCIPLINE

If a teacher routinely fails to get to lessons on time, this can seriously undermine class discipline. When the student comes to understand, even from a cursory reading of the *Kitzur*, how strict an obligation the teacher has to keep to the schedule—this being G-d's work—but sees that there is little correlation between the ideal and the reality—the effect is to erode his own capacity for discipline, weakening his grasp on other principles in the *Shulchan Aruch*, since all are part of one grand design. The student, feeling how much his own school day is ruled by the clock, is the involuntary witness to the teacher's *disregard* of it. The upshot is that the class, which has by now passed sentence on him, will stop taking the teacher seriously. What point will there be then, later on, in exhorting students to greater diligence?

Getting to class on time is, indeed, the *sine qua non* of a sound education, quite apart from the fact that it is an explicit halachic obligation codified in the *Shulchan Aruch*.

WHERE IS RESPONSIBILITY?

How can a teacher, who presumably believes in what he is doing, be late for class? Where is his sense of responsibility for the Torah study neglected by his students, for their precious time that he has squandered? Surely this qualifies as "doing G-d's work in a fraudulent manner!" And where is his fear of Heaven, if he is able brazenly to disregard an explicit *halacha* in the *Shulchan Aruch*?

Optimal Use of Lesson Time

The teacher must make optimal use of class-time—not just going through the motions, but giving the lesson rich and satisfying content.

Being Prepared—Something to Build Upon

The teacher who arrives in class on time but without having prepared his material in a systematic manner—is the thief of the student's time. Had he prepared himself properly, no theft would have occurred, his students would have got much more out of the allotted time, and the lesson would have been truly productive.

These strictures apply regardless of the make-up of the class, regardless of the ease or difficulty of the topic—we *must* be prepared beforehand.

Doing G-d's Work with Inner Conviction

To whom should we compare the teacher who does not prepare his or her material thoroughly and well?—to parents who give their child food that is only half-cooked, or rotten. We know all too well that the lack of good and nourishing food can stunt the growth and the development of the child, and how much more so the child's faculties and talents; and it is not hard to foresee the baneful effects in later years of the failure to receive sound nutrition in childhood.

The above is true to an even greater degree when it comes to education. The development of the student's abilities depends to a great extent upon the manner of instruction—how the teacher prepared the lesson, how he or she presented and explained the material—and upon the grounding that the student is given. If its preparation, and the way the material was imparted, were not all they should have been, and this state of affairs is allowed to persist—the consequences for the child will emerge in later life, when he or she will be afflicted, G-d forbid, with something not unlike spiritual atrophy.

An educator must do his work—which, as we have said—is the work of G-d, with *emunah*, in good faith, and not just by conforming to externals—getting to class punctually, and so on. Rather, there must be an inner conviction, evident in the way in which he stretches the student to his or her limits—and this, by dint of good preparation and proper explanation. Absent this— even if he is as punctual as the nine o' clock news—he belongs in the category of "one who acts deceitfully in the performance of G-d's work," stealing and withholding from the student that which he or she should rightfully have received from him.

A LOSS THAT CAN NEVER BE MADE GOOD

As is well-known, the law prohibits public-sector workers from going on strike. When, as sometimes happens, they rebel against these constraints, what form does their action take? The answer is that they turn up to work and "go-slow." And to protest is futile since, when all is said and done, they have turned up for work, and we cannot deny that they *are* working!

We all know how much disruption this so-called work can cause; sometimes it is more damaging than an actual strike!

Now you will sometimes find in the case of a *melamed* that, yes, he too turned up to class, but that in fact the teaching was carried out in the spirit outlined above. Again—not to mince words—this counts as "doing G-d's work fraudulently"; it is ruinous for the student and it cheats him of his time, a loss that can never be made good. Where, we ask, where is the fear of Heaven?

CHAPTER 7
RELIGIOUS STUDIES

THE BEGINNING OF A NEW PROGRAM OF STUDY

When the students embark upon a new program of learning, for example: the beginning of *Siddur*, of *Chumash*, of *Mishnayot*; an introduction to, or a new chapter in, Talmud—this occasion should be marked with the festive atmosphere suited to such an important "transition." Accordingly, an invitation should be extended to parents, as well as to the Rabbi, the *menahel* of the school, and so on; and there should be a *seudat* mitzvah. We are starting something new!

This will raise the student to a new level where Torah-learning becomes something spontaneous and joyful—the fact that he or she is learning Torah will become, in itself, cause for rejoicing. To begin *Gemara* learning, for example, with a celebration—gives the young student tangible evidence of the difference between this kind of mental activity and, say, the study of mathematics. His learning will take on special meaning for him, and he will bring to it an extra measure of zest and earnestness.

WINE OF TORAH

During *Chumash* study-time, we should do our best to highlight some point derived from a particular verse and elaborated upon in Chasidic teachings, so that, during the reading of the Torah, that point will be reinforced for the student when the *baal koreh* comes to the relevant verse.

BAAL HA-TURIM

It is a good idea to expose the children from time to time to some of the nuances of interpretation found in the *Baal ha-Turim*, which brings out the richness and hidden complexities of the Torah, and which can bring us to a loftier appreciation of all that Torah is, to an abiding interest in the letters which compose it and their *g'matriot*, and in comparing the expressions and words of the Torah, and so on.

FLUENCY IN SCRIPTURE

The children must be given the ability readily to recite and translate any part of Scripture *l'girsah*, so that fluency and instant recognition are achieved—in other words, when they see a verse, they will recognize it at once, particularly a verse in *Chumash* and *Tehillim*. This will only be accomplished by frequent textual review and, where practical, memorization.

The children must be urged to fix a time every day for the learning of *Chumash* by heart, so that over time they will become thoroughly versed in it. Beyond this, there is a variety of methods that can be employed to improve skills and put mastery within reach of everyone.

REVIEWING AT HOME

In every *parsha* we should find something that has a practical application, draw the students' attention to this aspect of the text, and be sure to have them review the material at home. In this way the Torah will be a living Torah—not study alone, but something that provides a spur and impetus to action.

This will bring bountiful blessings—to the institution, to the students, to the parents.

STUDY OF *NACH*

Comparatively little time is devoted to the study of *Nach* and it will not come as a surprise that knowledge of it is inadequate. There has to be at the very least a general level of knowledge of *Nach*, and familiarity with it, so that when a child sees or hears a verse, he should instantly be able to identify the prophet who gave voice to it.

I strongly recommend that a survey be conducted among the students to clarify—first: what books of *Nach* they have studied up till now—second: whether they in fact know the names of all twenty-four books of *Tanach*.

LEARNING OF *TEHILLIM*

In those classes in which the *Sefer Tehillim* is studied, what makes most sense is for them to learn the chapters that we recite in prayer. In this way they will broaden their study of *Nach*, as well as their knowledge of the meaning of the text of the *tefillah*.

DAILY *GEMARA*

One of our priorities must be to ensure that the children devote at least two full hours a day to the study of *Gemara*, and that these should be the *first* two hours of the day.

If it proves to be impractical to organize this study for two hours continuously, then the hours may be divided—one in the morning and an additional hour after other subjects (for example, *Navi* and *halacha*), but *not* after the secular subjects.

MEMORIZATION OF *MISHNAH*

The learning of *Gemara*—right across the board—should begin only *after* the memorization of *Mishnah*. There is a sound basis to this:

First and foremost: the simple activity of learning and knowing *mishnayot* by heart.

Second—this will, logically enough, assist with the study of the *Gemara*, since the *Gemara* cites part of the *mishnah* and explains it, and if the student is not perfectly at home in the *Mishnah*—he cannot expect to master the *Gemara*. Knowing the *Mishnah* by heart, on the other hand, will contribute greatly to the understanding of the *Gemara*.

Third—after studying the explanation of the *Mishnah* provided by the *Gemara*, he should review the *Mishnah* in the light of that explanation, and when the student knows the *Mishnah* by heart, this will help him remember the analysis of it found in the *Gemara*.

LEARNING THE *MISHNAYOT* OF THE ENTIRE *PEREK*

The preferred method of learning *Gemara* is to study at the outset the *mishnayot* of the entire *perek*. When the student sees how the *Gemara* analyzes and explains the material of the *mishnah*, he will discover a new approach to learning.

SHULCHAN ARUCH

Halachot should be learned in the *Kitzur Shulchan Aruch* (and not in new *seforim*, such as *Sefer Halichot Olam*). The student should also be taught how to "find his bearings" in this *sefer*.

[The student must be given to understand that wherever there is a difference in point of law or emphasis between the

Kitzur and the *Shulchan Aruch* of the Alter Rebbe, we follow the latter.*

Where it is possible to study the *Shulchan Aruch* of the Alter Rebbe, this should be done.]

KEY *HALACHOT*

Efforts must be made to organize among the students the learning of key *halachot*, in *Orach Chayim*—something which the Rebbe has called for on many occasions. The most effective approach is to set up pairs of students, each pair working on a different *halacha*, the aim being to acquire a clear and detailed understanding of it.

MUSSAR (ETHICS)

The Rebbe takes the view that in places where there is no possibility of learning *Chasidus*, the study of *mussar* is the next best thing. For in everything that is learned one must find pointers to the more exalted service of G-d, and this is precisely the function of the educator and teacher. Clearly, not every educator is equipped for such a task; therefore, one solution would be for every school to have a teacher whose special responsibility is to visit classes at intervals and address them on *mussar* topics.

THE HISTORY OF THE JEWISH PEOPLE

We expect every student to have at least a general knowledge of the history of the Jewish People—to know the dates of

---

* Recently, a *Kitzur Shulchan Aruch* containing the rulings of the Alter Rebbe has been published by the Kehot Publication Society.

the prophets, the kings, the *Tannaim*, the *Amoraim*, the *Geonim*, the *Rishonim*, and so on.

I recall that one student was asked when the *Rambam* lived— a hundred years ago? a thousand? or at the time of the Talmud?—he had not the least idea!

Sometimes teachers, never mind their students, are not as well up in these subjects as they ought to be, and are in no position to teach them. I would urge the teachers to use their vacation time to "bone up" on them, and qualify themselves to teach them. Alternatively, there might be one teacher whose knowledge is sufficiently broad-based to enable him or her to teach several classes.

PENMANSHIP

It is important to devote one hour a week to the cultivation of good handwriting—to train the children to write nicely and clearly and to form the letters correctly. We find children distorting the Hebrew characters so badly that what they write is illegible. Similarly, they make far too many mistakes when they write in Hebrew. There was a saying once: "They write the word Noach with seven mistakes!" but now they've managed to exceed even that number!

It's known how exacting the Rebbeim were when it came to writing, as elaborated on by Rabbi Yosef Yitzchak of Lubavitch in his *sichot*. Taking care to write nicely and clearly—can have its effect upon the character, develop a feeling for beauty, for order and for neatness.

Any progress in this area would also exert a positive influence on the parents.

A *SIYUM*

Generally speaking, the custom of holding a class celebration at the completion of a specific section of study is limited to that of an entire Tractate (of the Talmud). However, there is room for more flexibility with younger students, and we can hold a celebration after the completion of a chapter, (before the *siyum* the students should learn the *mishnayot* in the chapter by heart). And with younger children—at the conclusion of one *parsha*, one Book of the Five Books of Moses, and so on. In the same way, we can hold a *siyum* at the end of the academic year in recognition of all the *mishnayot* that were learned and memorized during the course of it.

Apart from the importance of the *siyum*, which endears the Torah to the student and raises its stature in his eyes, the parents will get to hear about it from their son and will no doubt mention it to their neighbors. This will give a boost to enrollment.

The children should come to the party in their *Shabbat* clothes. It's best if the event takes place in the afternoon, so that parents can also attend.

Chapter 8
THE FEMALE STUDENT

THE DRESS CODE

The students must be left in no doubt as to what makes for modesty in dress. Similarly, very great care must be taken to avoid situations of *yichud*, (seclusion with a member of the opposite sex not of one's close family), in accordance with the *halacha*.

THE BREACH INVITES THE THIEF

A young girl must be given to understand that behavior unbecoming the modesty of the daughters of Israel will place her in the way of temptation, and that sooner or later she will find herself in a situation over which she has no control. Our Sages were thinking specifically of this when they stated, (*Succah*, 26a): "The breach invites the thief." However, these problems originate in early childhood, when proper attention was not paid to this subject and the proper attitudes inculcated.

"CAUSING THE MULTITUDE TO STRAY"

When a student behaves immodestly—she becomes a provocation to the onlooker, and there is no telling where things may lead. Whatever the cause, with her remains the responsibility for what ensues, even if nothing could have been further from her mind.

When discussing modesty, this concept—"causing the multitude to stray"—should be thoroughly explored.

THE TEMPTATION OF THE GENERATION

Every generation possesses a form of idolatry peculiar to the age, and which it has to make a special effort to overcome and destroy. In our generation we are being assailed by the forces of immodesty, which we must take all necessary measures to guard against and repel.

In this connection, it is commonly found that where an individual has repeatedly sinned, habit has, so to speak, issued him a license to continue in this path, (*Yoma*, 86b), yet the prohibition remains in force.

PUBLIC MARCHES, FUND-COLLECTING

It was brought to our attention in a memorandum that girls from one of the schools took part in a street procession. We do not, as a general rule, view this favorably. It does not reflect well upon the character of the daughters of Israel, of whom it is written: "All the honor of the king's daughter is within," (*Tehillim*, 45:14). The same stricture applies where girls go house-to-house collecting money for charity, and other good causes.

Let the distinction between this and the *Lag B'omer* Parade, and other such processions, be absolutely clear: the whole point and purpose of the parade is the strengthening of Judaism—which is not at all the case with the ordinary kind of march, or with door-to-door collections.

Curricular Recommendations to Schools*

The curriculum for the girls should include the following:

A: Specific topics from "Duties of the Heart," the section "Gate of Understanding."

B: Various aspects of *hashkafa*, from "Gates of Understanding, of Rabbeinu Yona.

C: Serious and intensive study of *Pirkei Avot*, whose subject is the fear of Heaven and the development of good character traits. Learning various sayings and aphorisms by heart.

D: How to check and how to kosher meat and fowl, in addition to study of the relevant laws.

E: How to bake *challah*, together with the laws of baking. In former times all the women of the house would bake *challah* for *Shabbat*. But even today, when *challot* are readily available in shops, we find that some parents do not take advantage of this; alternatively, they may find themselves in a location where they are not available.

F: Our goal is to help our students build a home among the Jewish people on the foundations of purity and sanctity. In order to forestall some of the marital problems that can be blamed upon the lack of proper guidance in earlier years, we must take it upon *ourselves* to provide such guidance.

G: To direct their path towards the care and the education of the young and the very young.

H: To provide them with formal instruction in hygiene.

I: There are girls who show a leaning toward a particular subject, such as history or accounting. Note should be taken of this and these girls given every encouragement, so that in the

---

* To the Lubavitch network of schools for underprivileged children in Israel.

course of time they will be able to impart this knowledge to others, as teachers and pedagogues.

J: To develop musical talents.

K: Sewing, and housecraft in all its aspects.

L: Wig styling.

M: As for learning foreign languages, perhaps Russian should be the priority—to facilitate communication with, and outreach to, those who are leaving Russia, with G-d's help.

CHAPTER 9
PUNISHMENT

PUNISHMENT IN AN EDUCATIONAL CONTEXT

If the recourse to punishment is indeed to be part of our educational approach, it should be for the sole purpose of producing in the student the conviction that he is being punished out of love and out of a concern for his future. Neither anger nor revenge but the desire to heal must be the motive if the punishment is to be effective—the student must feel that the object is not to cause him or her pain but to teach a necessary lesson. To this end, the nature of the student's offense should be made clear at the very moment that the punishment is being meted out.

When the punishment takes the form of memorization or copying—what is memorized or copied should bear some relationship to the student's offense—for obvious reasons.

The teacher or principal must deliberate long and hard before taking the decision to punish the child—out of consideration for the fact that the adult this child will in due course become, may at some point also find himself in the role of teacher or educator of Jewish children. In that role, he may be in a position to impose punishment, (and perhaps have an unconscious compulsion to do so).

EXPULSION FROM THE CLASSROOM/SCHOOL

As a general rule, students should not be put out of the classroom. However, if there is absolutely no alternative, they may be transferred to another class, or kept occupied in the classroom. There are several factors at work here:

Firstly, when a student is turned out of the class and sent home, he or she will experience this as a form of exile, in connection with which the *halacha* states: "When a student is exiled, his teacher must be exiled with him," (*Makkot*, 10a). Has the teacher really understood all the implications of his action?

Secondly, the teacher's responsibility for the students extends beyond the walls of the classroom—does his behavior convey awareness of this? (If not, the savvier of the students will observe that the teacher is ignoring, or acting in ignorance of, the *halacha* that deals with the expulsion of students, and appears to be shirking his responsibilities... Naturally, they will take a dim view of the whole business!)

Thirdly, one who teaches his neighbor's child is looked upon as if he himself has begotten him, and what parents will have the heart to cast out their children?—*We don't throw our children onto the street.* How, then, can a teacher bring himself to throw his student-child out of the classroom?!

CORPORAL PUNISHMENT

In an earlier generation, it was not unknown for a teacher to give a student a *patsch*—a light smack. Nowadays, however, (unless the teacher who does so is certain that he is doing it for the good of the student, and not just to vent his own anger—) this is forbidden, absolutely forbidden, since we are not allowed to strike a fellow Jew.

Experience has taught that laying one's hands on a student has only negative effects. We should therefore renounce the practice completely.

PRESSURE—OUT OF LOVE

We must drive a student, and exert pressure on him or her, only to the extent that wisdom dictates, taking pains at the same time to persuade the student that we are acting in his or her best interests. Over time the student will come to understand that it is love that turns the teacher into such a hard taskmaster.

Pressure brought to bear by one who is well disposed to us does not register as pain.

The greater the pressure—the greater the love must be.

KNOWING WHEN TO STOP

When a teacher finds himself obliged to punish or come down hard on a student, it must only be for the good of the student, with no ulterior motive whatsoever. But even then, it must be within measure. Losing sight of this fact constitutes a breach of the prohibition against "oppressing one's friend," viz. not to oppress another Jew in speech, (*Behar*, 25:17; *Kitzur Shulchan Aruch*, 63:1).

We find that, in the case of corporal punishment, the teacher who is overzealous transgresses a negative commandment—since he is using physical force without authority, he is no better than one who strikes, or raises his hand to strike, another Jew! (*Hilchot Talmud Torah* of the Alter Rebbe, 1:13). And we find a parallel to this in the laws of *malkot* (lashes—imposed by the *bet din*), that just one stroke of the lash in excess of the prescribed number transgresses a negative commandment, (*Rambam, Hilchot Sanhedrin*, 16:12).

TEARS OF CONTRITION

The aim should be to bring the student to tears over what he or she has done, (but in a "loving manner"), for this is a true sign of contrition.

LETTING THE STUDENT CHOOSE

There are times when it should be left to the student himself, or herself, to decide the punishment that best fits their transgression.

REPRIMANDS

We have the obligation of "You shall surely reprimand your friend," (*Kedoshim*, 19:17), but we must fulfil it as the Torah would have us do so, in accordance with the *Shulchan Aruch*, and not, G-d forbid, by committing the sin of embarrassing someone in public. It is folly to think that a reprimand may be given through preaching or vexation of the spirit—rather, it is the demonstration of what is wrong in so clear a manner that the student is obliged to acknowledge the truth.

CHAPTER 10
ORPHANS

THE RESPONSIBLE PARTY

Orphans have a very special claim upon our attention and we must be ready to help and assist them in every conceivable way. Over and above the efforts of their own teachers, the welfare of these children should be the responsibility of one particular individual in each school. This is a sacred trust, for the teacher from whom the child learns Torah is looked upon as his second father, and if the teacher does not fulfil this role, who will?

The above applies most especially to those periods when school is not in session, such as Shabbat, festivals and the summer vacations.

A SPECIAL RAPPORT

"In our conduct towards orphans we must be scrupulous ... only speak to them with gentleness, never fail to show them respect, never wound them be it only with words, for their souls have been humbled and their spirits brought very low." (*Kitzur Shulchan Aruch*, 29:30).

We must be mindful to behave towards orphans with sensitivity and tact, for dejection dogs them at their heels. What others take for granted they must learn to live without, and awareness of this weighs heavily on their hearts.

Such children yearn for closeness and acceptance. We must therefore reach out to them and embrace them with warmth and openness—the blessings that flow from this will be incalculable. Teachers, therefore, must go to great lengths to involve themselves with such children, by inviting them to their homes, devising treats for them, and so on.

HELP AND ASSISTANCE

There are orphans who might clearly benefit from a move to another institution, where conditions are more likely to suit them, but have no one to act on their behalf. In such cases, the obligation to do so belongs to the principal, (as well as to the community in general).

Similarly, we must not overlook the question of material assistance. In the case of younger children, this may amount to no more than a pittance, although with the older child we can expect more substantial sums to be involved—something that parents would normally take care of.

It is essential that this help and assistance continue even after the children leave elementary school. We must ease their path through times of difficulty: guiding them through the crises of adolescence, promoting their academic studies, helping them to find a mate.

(The truth is, one would have expected the *rabbonim* in the Holy Land to take this upon themselves—to search out orphans and set up a body devoted exclusively to their needs).

THE ONE-PARENT FAMILY

There is a class of children, not unlike orphans, known as "orphans of the living." These are children from broken homes, a phenomenon which in this age has reached calamitous proportions. These children are *virtual* orphans, and sometimes their situation is a good deal worse than that of their partners in misfortune.

The plight of these children cries out for a comprehensive response on our part—given that the order of their day and indeed of their lives deviates so painfully from that of their peers, who are blessed with two parents. When both parents are on the scene there are in general two lines of force: "the left rebuffs and the right brings closer," according to the role each parent plays. In normal circumstances, when one takes the left side, the other takes the right, with the result that there is a balance of forces acting on the child. When, however, one of the parents no longer plays an active role, there is but one line, and one line only, it matters not which—it is a sorry state of affairs. This is especially so when the single parent has to worry about making ends meet, and is always having to deal with the many problems that such a life presents. The unfortunate outcome is that the child loses its bearings completely and goes through the whole day under a dark cloud.

The education of these children requires us to exert ourselves in quite specific ways, (a child without a father, for instance, should be invited by his teacher to accompany him to the synagogue).

Apropos "problem children"—a spokesman for the Israeli Department of Education announced only recently that in Israel there are almost twenty thousand children wandering the streets. In my opinion, the true figure is more than forty thousand!

CHAPTER 11

THE STUDENT AT HOME

THE MITZVAH OF WASHING HANDS

We must teach the children to pay more attention to the mitzvah of washing the hands in the morning, so that while they themselves are scrupulous in this respect they will also do their best to influence their parents and younger siblings. They must realize that this mitzvah is to be observed even on the days when they do not come to school, as on *Shabbat* and festivals, and vacation time.

"SLEEPING WITH TORAH"

We should get students of twelve and upwards into the habit of studying a paragraph from the *Shulchan Aruch*, etc. for several minutes before reciting the Shema at bedtime. In this way it will become second nature for them to fall asleep while occupied with Torah, a practice that will transform their sleeping hours and the entire day that follows. Similarly, younger students should fall asleep after reading, or having read to them, stories of *tzaddikim*.

THE EVENING PRAYER, THE RECITING OF *SHEMA*

The teacher must find out whether or not the students are reciting the evening prayer and the *Shema* at bedtime, and make a great to-do about this, especially for the benefit of the younger ones.

However, the teacher should not assume that just because he has already brought the matter to their attention he will not need to do so again. Now that the child is older, if in earlier days he recited only part of the bedtime *Shema*, he should now attempt it in its entirety. In the same vein, he should also demand more of himself. A further consideration is that other children may have joined the class who may never have been "challenged" on this point.

A questionnaire might be in order. All the students should describe what they do when they are not on the school premises—with respect to the evening prayer and *Shema* at bedtime, for example. The parents should then sign the document.

MAKING A DIFFERENCE AT HOME

We should be encouraging the children, even from the earliest years, to do what they can, however indirectly, to exert an influence in the home. This is not a matter of outreach alone, rather it goes to the heart of the child's education that the atmosphere in the home should augment in the best way possible what takes place in the school.

We must try to influence the older children along the same lines, and try to implant in them a sense of responsibility towards their younger brothers and sisters.

THE MITZVAH CAMPAIGNS

The teacher should make efforts to ensure that in the student's home there is active involvement with all of the ten mitzvah campaigns announced by the Lubavitcher Rebbe—for example:

THE MEZUZA CAMPAIGN

The details of the *kashrut* of *mezuzot* must be explained to the students. We should also inspect the *mezuzot* in their homes.

In Riga, The Rebbe, Rabbi Yosef Yitzchak of Lubavitch, was heard to say that putting on invalid *tefillin* is far more serious than not putting them on at all, since one who puts on invalid *tefillin* is under the impression that he has fulfilled his duty, whereas one who neglects to do so has the feeling that all is not as it should be. The same is true of invalid *mezuzot*.

We must also impress upon the students that whenever they see a mezuzah they should give a moment's thought to the intention of the words written there.

THE *KASHRUT* CAMPAIGN

It should be possible, (during home visits and the like), to help parents understand the importance of *kashrut*—looked at from a purely human point of view.

It is a given that parents want the very best for their child, and have no conscious desire to rob him of freedom of action in the future, or to undermine in any way his ability to choose a life of Torah and *mitzvot*. And yet, if while at a tender age he is fed non-kosher food, which turns into his own flesh and blood and dulls his body and spirit, how can we prevent the situation developing later on in life in which it becomes infinitely more difficult for him to choose a life of Torah!

THE MITZVAH CAMPAIGNS AND *CHINUCH*

There are educators who take the view that the mitzvah campaigns do not necessarily represent a personal call to action, since they are already involved in the holy work of the Almighty; moreover, they suspect that there may be a conflict between the work of *chinuch* and the demands of the campaigns.

The truth, is, however, that there is a direct correlation between the mitzvah campaigns and the educational enterprise in general.

First, every teacher is interested in having students come to the school from a home which observes family purity, keeps a kosher kitchen and has kosher *mezuzot*; a home where, in his spare time, the father occupies himself with Torah study. Clearly these are things which nourish the character and the abilities of the student, in ways that will benefit the educational process itself: its standards, the tenor and tempo of study, its overall effectiveness.

Secondly, the teacher who is involved in the mitzvah campaign becomes a role model for his students, they see that he is himself working for the good of others, out of selflessness and love of his fellow Jew, and will be inspired to emulate his example.

Thirdly, "one who teaches his neighbor's son Torah is looked upon as if he begot him"—it clearly follows that it is up to the teacher to concern himself with the domestic situation of his student-son, this being one of his obligations.

Fourthly, this activism will create a rapport between teacher and parent, something which can only help give a tremendous boost to the education of the student.

Concern for Every Detail

Parents leave nothing to chance when it comes to providing for the health needs of their children—nutrition, quality of air, whatever is vital for the child. It is no different when it comes to the *spiritual* health of the student—the educator must concern himself with what goes on in his student's home, and what the student does while he is there, overlooking nothing. By the same token he must look for ways to effect changes where change is called for.

His interest must extend to the question of the observance of *kashrut* and *Shabbat* in the house, the state of the *mezuzot*, and so on, to the last detail—he must be concerned to verify that everything is on a par with the education the child is receiving in the institution.

If for whatever reason the teacher is prevented from collaborating with the parents of the children to improve home conditions—the responsibility and the meritoriousness lie with him to ensure that somebody else acts in his place.

If conditions in the student's home are in fact far from ideal—the case can be made that it is the educator's job to take the student under his wing and watch over him every single hour of the day!

Home Visits

The teacher must seize the opportunity to visit the student's family, in order to become acquainted with his home and neighborhood. If the student has specific difficulties of an intellectual or behavioral kind, the teacher will, as a result of his visits, be in a stronger position to pinpoint the causes—domestic, environmental, etc.—the better to decide what steps need to be taken on the student's behalf.

CHAPTER 12
PRAYER

EXEMPLARS OF PRAYER

Children cannot be expected to treat the synagogue as a place of reverence and awe unless the adults in their lives also do so. For the child, the synagogue must be the place where prayer is found in its purest and most intense form. When these conditions are met, he should have no trouble learning how to pray in a proper manner: audibly; with a tranquil spirit; without yielding to distraction; without straying from his place. Most importantly, it simply will not occur to him to talk during prayer, and especially during the *chazzan's* repetition and the Reading of the Torah.

PREPARATION FOR PRAYER

The Rebbe, (see *sicha* of *Rosh Chodesh Marcheshvan*, 5642-1981), would frequently remind us of the ruling in the *Shulchan Aruch (Orach Chaim*, beginning of Section 98), to the effect that, by way of preparation for prayer, one must meditate on the loftiness of the Almighty and the lowliness of man. However, in order to achieve its goal, this meditation must be translated into emotional reality, something that does not happen instantaneously. The Rebbe has expressed surprise that so many people should appear oblivious to this, and dismay, that no one is calling attention to the need for a heightening of awareness on this very point.

This is a matter of practical *halacha*. We must change the reality, and to do this we must organize classes, for students and for laymen. These classes should deal with the laws applicable to each and every prayer, and authoritative works dealing with these topics should be consulted. At every point, it goes without saying, the material should be suited to the level of the student, and vice-versa.

There must be a concerted effort to raise the level of prayer.

VOCAL HOPSCOTCH

Among the students there are those who skip, or elide and slur over the letters of the prayers. We find this particularly among the brighter students, who often escape scrutiny for that reason. However, we must be on the lookout for this and try to reverse the trend.

Once the Rebbe was moved to point out to me a certain boy in the *minyan* in "770," who appeared to be garbling his prayers and needed to be taken aside and spoken to. This particular boy was very young, yet the Rebbe felt unable to overlook the matter. If this is the case, it certainly behooves the parents and the teachers to do something practical themselves.

It cannot be emphasized strongly enough that prayer should be a real "happening," something that we do well and take pride in, regardless of the grades of the classes, and especially in the junior and senior *yeshivot*. And quite apart from prayer, which is the heart of the matter, we can expect any improvement to have many positive "spin-offs," affecting other areas of activity.

CONCENTRATION IN PRAYER

Every day in our prayers we recite the words from the *Mishnah*, *Eilu D'varim*, among them, *iyun t'filah*—concentration in prayer. One who is unable to maintain concentration throughout the prayers should at least say one paragraph, one psalm or one verse as it should be said, with energy and conviction. In this way there will be at the very least one complete prayer that has been salvaged, as it were, from an entire year of prayers, and that merits the designation "concentration in prayer."

REQUESTING ONE'S NEEDS

A child knows that if it craves something it has to request it of a person with the power to grant the request. In the same way, we must bring the child up to know that everything is in the hands of G-d, and that if it needs or wants something badly it must request it of G-d, who hears the prayers of the whole world. And when it requests it in truthfulness—the request will be granted. It follows, then, that prayer should take the form of a request for one's needs to be satisfied—uttered, accordingly, in the spirit with which one requests something of a human being: with sincerity and earnestness.

FLUENCY IN PRAYER

We must go about familiarizing the students with the daily prayers so that they are fluent in them.

THE MEANING OF THE WORDS

The meaning of the words of the prayers in their translated form should be taught in every department of the school—no student is too young, and no student too old, to benefit from this. Such knowledge will help him or her concentrate during prayer, and lend the prayer experience greater immediacy and "relevance."

The Rebbe the "Tzemach Tzedek" was known to test his grand-children on the meaning of the words of the prayers, (*Hayom Yom*, 8 Tevet).

The student must certainly be well acquainted with the meaning of the section on the various sacrifices, which is recited daily, before the prayer proper. (This recital is in place of the sacrificial offering, hence its importance). The same requirement extends to the chapter dealing with the positions on the altar of the various sacrifices, recited by way of Torah learning before the prayer, and as a preparation for it. (It is anyone's guess what proportion of the students really knows the meaning of this chapter!) And finally, the *beraitha* of Rabbi Yishmael, setting out the thirteen principles of Torah interpretation.

ANALYSIS OF PRAYER

Once a week, students at all levels should be taught the interpretation and explanation of a specific section in the order of the prayers—with the idea of covering all of them over the course of time. With all due allowance for the age of the students, the text should be delved into and explicated, enabling them to draw out a practical lesson capable of application to their daily lives.

In this way the student will arrive at a proper appreciation of prayer, the actual experience of which will take place at a higher and more enlightened level. (There is, moreover, the obvious pedagogic benefit of living by what is recited day-in, day-out).

Particular emphasis should be given to Scriptural verses which speak of the love of Torah and of its sublime character: "The Torah of G-d is perfect, restoring the soul," for example. A psalm that should certainly be studied is *"Barchi Nafshi,"* which opens up for the child or student a broad perspective on the greatness of G-d in the natural world.

AFFECTING THE ENTIRE DAY

We see evidence of this all the time: when a student starts the day by praying with a spirit of serenity, and recites the prayers in the proper manner, he becomes a different person for the rest of the day. For the plain truth is that the earnest involvement with prayer has a profound influence on the student's actions and on his fear of G-d.

NOT TO PASS IN FRONT OF SOMEONE AT PRAYER

The law that prohibits passing in front of someone at prayer seems to be widely ignored. The students must be taught to respect this law and must be seen to respect it.

THE VERSE CORRESPONDING TO ONE'S NAME

The students should be instructed to recite—at the conclusion of the *Amidah* Prayer—the Biblical verse corresponding to their name.

THE CHAPTER OF PSALMS CORRESPONDING TO ONE'S AGE

The students should be taught the custom of saying the chapter of Psalms corresponding to their age, (a ten-year old will say the eleventh Psalm, and so on). In addition, they should learn the chapter and have an understanding of its content. If they begin to do this while they are young, the habit will remain with them for the rest of their life.

In the classroom, also, the chapters corresponding to the age of the students, (usually, not more than two chapters), should be studied.

The Rebbe's chapter should also be studied.

PRAYER WITH A *MINYAN*

The students must be reminded that even outside of school they must pray with a *minyan*. It should be pointed out that this obligation is in force three times a day, and that the *Shulchan Aruch*, (*Kitzur Shulchan Aruch*, 12:8), mandates praying with a *minyan* located anywhere up to 3½ miles' walking distance from one's home or place of residence.

An incidental benefit: sometimes, when a father sees that his son makes a point of always getting to a *minyan*, he may well motivate himself to follow his son's example, on a more regular basis.

We also need to elaborate on the solid virtues of communal prayer:

Firstly, it is always acceptable and pleasing in the eyes of Heaven, (*Kitzur Shulchan Aruch*, 12:7), to the point where the virtue that is a conspicuous feature of prayer during the Ten Days of Penitence is regarded as a *conventional* feature of communal prayer during the rest of the year, (*Rosh Hashana*, 18a).

Secondly, if he is the one to complete the *minyan*, he accrues to himself the credit for having helped make the prayer of the others more acceptable.

Thirdly, when he prays earnestly, his earnestness stands him, and those who pray with him, in good stead, making their prayers that much more acceptable.

Conversely, we must show how serious a thing it is to pray with a *minyan*. It is analogous to a petition that one of the communities in the realm presents to the king, and to the effect it has upon him when he sees that the name of one of his subjects does not appear in the list of signatories.

So it is that the non-participation of the individual detracts from the merit of the group as a whole.

THE SANCTITY OF THE SYNAGOGUE

We must help the students to acquire a proper sense of the sanctity of the synagogue and of the awe that they should feel every time they enter it. The words of the Psalm (5:8), "But I, through Your abundant kindness, will enter Your house; I will bow down toward Your Holy Sanctuary in awe of You," will bring home to the students how much the atmosphere of the House of G-d, this place where the Divine Presence dwells, should stir their own emotions, and how vital a place the synagogue should be in their own lives.

We must deepen the respect in which they hold the synagogue. Children must not mistake it for a playground, a place where they can run about and amuse themselves as they please. Parents, teachers and *gabbaim* must all do their part to ensure that children learn this lesson at an early age.

On more than one occasion the Rebbe has felt obliged to dwell on the respect due to the synagogue. In a similar vein, we have watched him forego his dignity and bend down to personally pick up a piece of litter from the floor of the *shul*.

PROPER BEHAVIOR

Educators must demand from the *gabbaim*, from those who occupy themselves with the affairs of the community, from rabbis, and from every G-d-fearing person, that they commit themselves to establish synagogue standards that will spare the children the disillusioning sight of adults acting in contempt of the principles that they are taught in school.

Every adult must accept upon himself a twofold obligation. First, he himself must behave properly in the synagogue; second, he must be aware of his responsibility towards the young. Aware, too, of the ease with which he can lead them astray—and that to do so is to commit spiritual murder, no less.

Now of all times, when we are searching for ways to increase our merits in order to hasten the Redemption—now is the time to rid ourselves of anything in our conduct that is *not* redeemable!

BETWEEN *MINCHAH* AND *MA'ARIV*

How do the children pass the time between *Minchah* and *Maariv*? This is a pressing question that concerns us all and calls for a concrete response.

EXPLANATIONS OF THE PRAYERS—A SAMPLE GUIDE

The children must have explained to them the order of topics enumerated in the *mishnah*, "*Eilu D'varim*," that is recited in conjunction with the morning blessings, and the reason why this *mishnah*, and no other, was selected for recital at the beginning of the day:

HONORING one's father and mother—When a person wakes up in the morning, immediately after saying the morning blessings, and before hastening to pray, he should ask himself what he can do for his parents, such as bringing them something to drink, (as we find in *Chazal*, [*Kiddushin*, 31b, the end of the page] "honor—by bringing them food and drink"), or attending to their other needs.

DOING deeds of kindness—Even when on the way to the synagogue, if one comes across a Jew who is in need of help, one should help him immediately.

This is illustrated in a well-known story concerning the Rebbe the "Tzemach Tzedek," who extended a loan to a Jew before starting to pray, (*Sefer HaMamarim*, 5711-1951, p. 153). What better way can there be to prepare for prayer!

RISING early to go to the synagogue—When a person has a great deal on his mind, business and other concerns, one of the first things to fall by the wayside is punctual attendance at *shul*. This won't do, he must still be punctual! (He will just have to get up earlier in the morning).

HAVING guests at one's table—Sometimes when we arrive in *shul* we see an unfamiliar face. We should introduce ourselves and ask him if everything is okay; for instance, he may have only just arrived in town, without having eaten; or perhaps he has other needs that make it difficult for him to concentrate on his *davening*.

VISITING the sick—Sometimes, when we are readying ourselves to pray, we notice that a familiar face is missing. At such times we should make inquiries and find out if anything is amiss. Perhaps the person absent is sick and needs treatment or other kinds of attention.

The synagogue is often the place where donations are solicited for a bridal fund, and where those present may be asked to participate in a funeral procession. Prayer may justifiably be postponed in all such cases since they cannot wait.

CONCENTRATION in prayer—One may erroneously think, that since he's working for the good of the community, and is engaged in matters of pressing importance, he has a "blanket exemption" from the requirement to pray with proper deliberation. The *mishnah*, however, teaches that he has no such exemption, and that he must pray with concentration at all times.

MAKING PEACE between friends—At the end of the service, one may run into former friends who have had a falling out over some matter, or meet with acquaintances who are involved in a dispute. One must do what one can to make peace between them.

BETWEEN MAN AND WIFE—Sometimes a person may involve himself in the above-mentioned matters at the expense of his own domestic harmony, which is left to fend for itself, so to speak. We must remind him that his relationship with his wife must not be jeopardized, that nothing justifies its neglect.

THE STUDY OF TORAH is equal to them all—The line of reasoning—that involvement in community affairs exempts one from certain requirements—"rabbinic decrees," for instance—may also lead him to neglect Torah study. The *mishnah* tells him unequivocally that no such exemption exists and that every free moment he has during the course of the day must be utilized for the study of Torah.

CHAPTER 13
THE STUDY OF TORAH

THE LAWS OF TALMUD TORAH

It is appropriate for our students to make a formal study of the laws of *Talmud Torah*—at the very least, the minimum found in the *Kitzur Shulchan Aruch*.

Additionally, they should know chapters 155 and 156 of the *Shulchan Aruch* of the Alter Rebbe, dealing with the fixing of times for the study of Torah: one session in the morning, one in the evening.

THE VOICE OF TORAH

When our Sages call for diligence in Torah learning the expression they use is, "His mouth should never cease from study," (*Shabbat*, 30b). The key term here is "mouth", implying that the material studied should be vocalized—literally "the voice of Torah." We find this idea explained in *Kitzur Shulchan Aruch*, (chap. 27:5), namely, that the obligation of Torah study is fulfilled precisely when the words are articulated, since "the utterance of the lips constitutes an action." (*Bava Metzia*, 90b).

NOT TO STAMMER

How does one truly fulfil the mitzvah of *Talmud Torah*? By being word-perfect, explains Rashi, (*V'etchanan*, 6:7), "...so that when you are asked a question you are able to respond without hesitation, and without hemming and hawing."

One cannot reach this stage simply by learning the halacha. Rather, it must be constantly reviewed and memorized until it is clear in all its details. Then, when asked a question, one will be able to respond with confidence and authority.

With this approach, when the student grows up he need never fear being embarrassed by the questions of his little brother!

To establish such a standard, we must keep the students "on their toes" with tests in halacha given at regular intervals. The awarding of prizes for the best efforts will add an extra incentive.

What we have said with regard to the student of course applies to his teachers. When teachers are asked a question the reply should be immediate. When, for example, a child is about to eat cereal and asks the teacher what blessing it should make, it does not exactly inspire confidence if the teacher has to consult a colleague before replying.

RESPECT FOR TORAH SCHOLARS

The students must be taught the *halachot* that explain in practical terms the respect due to *talmidei chachamim*. When the student understands what it is to honor and respect a Torah scholar, the Torah itself will acquire greater prestige in his eyes, and this will spur him to devote himself to its study.

When a Torah scholar's travels bring him to our vicinity, he should be invited to address the students. The students can then be given a practical demonstration of the honor to be accorded him.

To the degree that the student comes to honor the Torah he will likewise honor the Torah scholar—the two states of mind are mutually reinforcing. First and foremost, though, he should honor and feel affection for his teacher and rabbi as the embodiment of an age-old authority.

The respect accorded to Torah scholars naturally gives rise to a more dynamic and creative connection with the Torah itself. And, down the line, we can look to an additional benefit: that the student's parents will feel joyful at the prospect of their child becoming part of the community of scholars.

"FOR THEY ARE OUR LIFE"

In times gone by there was the feeling, especially among chasidim, that everything one learned in the Torah, (from the word *"hora'ah,"* instruction), had direct relevance to oneself. Indeed, how could it be otherwise! The Torah was an integral part of the life of the Jew, it was the oxygen that he breathed. Everyone knew that the words of Torah "are our life and the length of our days," that, in the words of Rabbi Akiva, (*Berachot*, 61b): "(It is) the ground of our being." Such a conviction gave birth to a community of feeling, and a *weltanschauung* for which we can find no adequate parallel in the modern age.

Indeed, I fear that in our days we no longer form part of this fraternity of feeling. The "spirit of Torah" is missing, the zeal for Torah that burns bright when Torah is studied *as Torah*, not as an intellectual discipline. In our days, it has come to resemble the study of any other form of wisdom. Given this state of affairs, we must find a way to bring this feeling back to life, make its acquaintance all over again, and develop it anew.

THE LOFTINESS OF TORAH

We must find ways to awaken the students to the greatness and the preciousness of Torah, to give them some conception of the love of Torah that once shone so brightly in our midst; we must help them to experience this at the level of the emotions, to get a *geshmak*—a relish—out of the act of learning Torah, (leaving aside the basic obligation to study it, deriving from the acceptance of the yoke of Torah). All the eloquence at our disposal should be devoted to this cause.

It is possible to explain the verses recited when the Torah scroll is taken out and returned and when held aloft, in like vein—in all of them we find G-d Himself praising the Torah.

We are greatly helped in this by the explanation given in *Chasidus* in regard to the potent effect of gazing upon the letters of Torah, that seeing the letters produces an effect upon the soul. The same idea is expressed in the talks of the Previous Rebbe—the extent to which we are invigorated at the time that the Ark is opened, (*Likkutei Dibburim*, Part 5, p. 454).

LOVE OF TORAH

The Rebbe has often quoted the words of the lullaby, "Torah is the best merchandise!" *This* is the feeling that we want our children to grow up with: the Torah as the object of their desire, the centerpiece of their affection.

A ROLE MODEL

Every educator should have fixed times for Torah study. Apart from its value in absolute terms, this is bound to make an impression upon the students, helping to inspire genuine dedication to Torah study.

CHAPTER 14
HALACHA
IN EVERYDAY LIFE

HONORING ONE'S PARENTS

We must combat the widespread and dismaying ignorance of the *halachot* of this mitzvah—by spelling out clearly and forcefully what the act of honoring one's mother and father entails; and particularly of *fearing* them, since this is a positive mitzvah of the Torah, contained in the verse, "One must fear one's parents," (*Kedoshim*, 18:3). (Additional material on this topic may be found in the *Sefer Charedim*, Chap. 4, 1-10).

Honoring one's parents, as we read daily in the *Mishnah*, "*Eilu D'varim*" in the morning *berachot*, belongs to that class of *mitzvot* for which no fixed measure is prescribed, (*sheh'ayn lahem shiur*). We must accordingly place tremendous weight on the fulfillment of the mitzvah in the hope that the students will truly excel in it and, by the force of their own example, inspire those around them to fulfil it too.

For this reason, the long summer days, when the children are in their parents' company a good deal more, and when, therefore, the mitzvah may truly come into its own, are of critical importance.

A VARIETY OF PRACTICAL BENEFITS

Aside from the obligation and the mitzvah to honor one's parents *per se*—and that it is incumbent upon the educator to train the student to perform *mitzvot*—there are additional factors to be reckoned with:

a) When a student brings his parents fully into his frame of reference, his education and training benefit from the fact, root, leaf and branch. (In general, every mitzvah that the student performs puts marrow into the educational process).

b) The parents will value the educational institution and its personnel more highly than they did before, leading to a broader range of cooperation between them.

c) We sometimes find parents deciding that a religious education simply makes too many demands of them. On the other hand, when they consider how much respect they are shown by their child, are reluctant to remove it from that institution.

d) When a child's relationship with his parents is marked by harmony and refinement, this fact cannot fail to impress the neighbors, and some at least will be motivated to send their young ones to a religious institution capable of turning out such fine students. In the same way, these parents will inform their near and dear ones of their decision, and yet more students will be added to the roll.

e) As the parents come to discover the importance and value of this mitzvah, they will give greater honor to their own elderly parents. Apropos, the Rebbe has spoken a great deal of the verse, "And he shall turn the heart of the fathers to the children," (*Malachi*, 3:24 and *Rashi*).

It is not uncommon for parents to ask their child to perform an act which entails a breach of *Shabbat* observance, and when the child refuses the parent's anger is aroused, resulting in bad feelings on both sides. If, however, during the rest of the week the child never fails to defer to its parent's wishes, the parent will realize that his or her authority is not being challenged and that the child's non-compliance stems only from concern for the holiness of *Shabbat*, not from any other cause.

WE HAVE ONLY ONE SET OF PARENTS

Sometimes it is necessary to enlighten children to the fact that as far as the fulfillment of *mitzvot* is concerned, they are not obliged to follow their parents' instructions blindly. But for all that, they must grasp the fact that the obligation to honor and fear them, even when the parent in question is a wicked person and a sinner, continues to apply (*Kitzur Shulchan Aruch*, 143:9). Our mother and father are the only parents we have, and through this obligation we are everlastingly bound to them.

TEFILLIN

Students who lay *tefillin* must be urged to have them checked regularly. Pains must be taken to ensure that the *tefillin* are kosher and a pleasure to gaze upon.

TZITZIT

We must seriously interest the students in the subject of *tzitzit* and of course make sure that they wear them; they should have at least two pairs of *tallit katan*, one to wear and "one for the laundry bag."

THE SANCTITY OF *SEFORIM*

Another area of concern is the sanctity of *sifrei kodesh*—holy books. The children have to know, for example, what may be placed on top of what.

Let us take the Rebbe for our inspiration, since he is fastidious in these matters. More than once, when noticing a book lying face down or inappropriately placed in a pile, he has stopped what he is doing and attended to it—in spite of the fact that his schedule is so tight that not a moment of his time is unaccounted for.

RESPECT FOR ONE'S TEACHER

The *halachot* governing the student-teacher relationship must be studied in detail with the students. Not that the teacher should give any thought about the honor due to him or herself, G-d forbid, but that *without* respect for the teacher the student will be incapable of receiving guidance of any kind.

BLESSINGS OVER THE ENJOYMENT OF FOOD

These blessings demand meticulous study, calling as they do for a knowledge of the precise formula applying to each kind of food. Wherever possible, the students should know the specific quantity that each *beracha* requires; and it should be remembered that this class of *berachot* is an absolutely regular part of everyday life. Of equal importance is the blessing made after we finish eating. At every farbrengen, without exception, the Rebbe would remind the gathering to make this blessing.

In addition, the students should know the Concluding Blessing, that is said after the "seven varieties"—wine, grapes, cake, etc.

THE BLESSING *ASHER YATZAR*

Let us ensure that all the students know this *beracha* by heart, and that they recite it at the proper time.

ONE-HUNDRED *BERACHOT* EVERY DAY

We must impress upon the students the importance of the *halacha* that requires at least one hundred *berachot* to be said every single day, (*Kitzur Shulchan Aruch*, 6:7). The importance attached to this mitzvah—as with all *mitzvot* of the Torah possessing a special virtue—is enhanced by the fact that it draws other *mitzvot* after it; for example, one is much less prone to forget the evening prayer when he is conscious of his obligation to complete the hundred blessings for that day. The same goes for other prayers and blessings.

When a teacher informs the students that on *Shabbat* we need to eat fruit if we are to reach the "magic number," (*Kitzur Shulchan Aruch*, ibid.), each student will ask his mother for fruit and she in turn will ask: "Why today, especially?" Her child will explain the obligation to recite the one hundred daily blessings and that on *Shabbat*—when certain weekday blessings are omitted, thereby diminishing the number—we make them up by eating fruit. In this way the student will succeed in making *Halacha* part of the domestic routine.

We should explain to the student that the blessings of the Reading of the Torah, recited every *Shabbat*, Monday and Thursday, also contribute to the total, and then he will feel more of a compulsion to be present at the Torah reading.

NOT TO DESTROY WANTONLY

This important prohibition reminds the students of, and sensitizes them, to the fact that everything in the world is part of G-d's plan, and for this reason one may not destroy anything without good cause. This knowledge will also strengthen their faith since it deepens their awareness of the Creator and Commander of the world.

We can underline this teaching with a story told by the Previous Rebbe, (*Likkutei Dibburim*, Part 1, p. 168). On one occasion he was walking with his father who was in the process of explaining a deep topic in *Chasidus*. Absent-mindedly, he plucked a leaf from a shrub and earned himself a gentle rebuke from his father.

RESPECTING OTHER PEOPLE'S PROPERTY

We must teach the students to respect and to be mindful of other people's property. A meaningful amount of time should be devoted to this. Summertime and vacation-spots are a prime focus of concern, demanding a much greater degree of awareness, (in the environmental sense, also)—for many adults, never mind children, relax their vigilance at such times, and in such places, allowing the distinction between what is theirs and what is not theirs to become blurred, and end up taking liberties with other people's property.

Everyone must acknowledge that "To G-d belongs the earth and its fullness," and that what He gives to others He gives for a particular reason, namely, that they should use it to fulfil His purposes. Now if I come along and help myself to what is not mine, I deny its owner the possibility of fulfilling the purpose for which it was granted to him in the first place, thereby frustrating the plan of Creation.

We must also stress that the prohibition against theft has not to do primarily with the monetary value of the article in question; the *issur* applies as much to to a princely sum as to a pittance—the total figure having relevance to the scale of the loss sustained by the injured party, but not to the prohibition itself.

We must also underline the point that the prohibition applies even in a case where we take what belongs to another but have every intention of returning it.

ERUVEI CHATZEROT

A number of lessons should be devoted to teaching the students the laws of *eruvei chatzerot*, (the combining of private domains on *Shabbat* in order to allow carrying from one domain to another), and also *eruvei t'chumin*, (it being prohibited to go beyond the city limits, in any direction, a distance greater than two thousand *amah*—between three to four thousand feet—although there exist circumstances in which to some degree, and with the correct procedure, circumvention of these limits is possible).

THE LAWS OF CHINUCH

The students should be taught the *halachot* of *chinuch*. When they begin to form an idea of the responsibilities of the educator and of the license that he or she is given to demand and expect the student's unquestioning obedience, they will surely respond to their teacher's words and instructions with more wholeheartedness and a better grace.

NOT TO MISUSE THE GIFT OF SIGHT

As to what our students feast their eyes upon—we must repeatedly caution them about the dangers that they face, for temptation lies in wait at every corner and the streets that they haunt assail their senses with images of unspeakable licentiousness. How many of them will succumb to the lure of the TV sets in shop-windows, or wherever else that they can see their fill of the images and scenes beamed out from them, at every hour of the day and night?

What we see engraves itself upon the mind and continues to affect us long after we have left the scene. *Chasidus* has much to say about this phenomenon: the great effect that the act of seeing, and the object seen, have upon the soul.

MITZVOT OF THE HEART

Most of the world has neither knowledge of, nor interest in this topic. It must therefore be rescued from the oblivion it has fallen into and be publicized as much as possible. (It is dealt with at length in the *Sefer Charedim*, under the above heading).

BETWEEN ONESELF AND ONE'S FELLOW

The manner in which we behave towards one another is a reliable gauge of our health both as a community and as a people. That said, what we are witness to at the present time is none too heartening. To take the charitable view, this may be owing to nothing more reprehensible than ignorance of the relevant *halachot*. Therefore, an intensive review of Chapter 156 in the *Shulchan Aruch* of the Alter Rebbe is called for. This, it is our pious hope, should go a long way towards rectifying the situation.

CHAPTER 15
FEAR OF HEAVEN

YIRAT SHAMAYIM

We are living in times of crisis. Our response must be to imbue our students even more deeply with the fear of Heaven and the acceptance of the yoke of the kingdom of G-d, and to do this as a matter of urgency!

I am obliged to point out that, on this score, many schools are not living up to their responsibility, which is borne out by the fact that when I ask principals:—"What are you doing to turn out students who are truly Heaven-fearing? How do you rate your efforts in this area?"—no answer is forthcoming.

We must put on the table for intensive and in-depth discussion everything connected with the fear of Heaven, and learn with the students *maamarim* devoted to this topic—never forgetting that the study of *halacha* can, in and of itself, bring us to the fear of Heaven.

We must launch a new campaign on the theme of *yirat shamayim*, combining rhetorical skills with a sophisticated knowledge of the media in order to give it maximum publicity—and to reach all age groups in the attempt. *Yirat shamayim* must become the burning issue, the hot topic of the day!

FOUNDATION OF THE WHOLE TORAH

Yirat shamayim is the foundation and the underpinning of the entire Torah. Nor should it be the least surprising that the fear of Heaven is the foundation of the *Shulchan Aruch*. In the *Kitzur Shulchan Aruch*, equally, the opening words read: "I have set G-d before me at all times"—this is *yirat shamayim*.

Of course, fear is a complex emotion: the fear of punishment, the fear of public opinion, and so on, but dominating all is the fear of Heaven itself.

FIRST THE FEAR OF SIN, THEN WISDOM

"When the fear of sin comes before wisdom, wisdom itself endures." (*Avot*, 3:9). The students must have a sure grasp of the truth of the *Mishnah*'s teaching that, by virtue of the fear of Heaven, "wisdom endures"—tempering such knowledge with the teaching of *Chasidus*, that together with fear must go an exultant joy—"trembling, co-existent with joy," (*Tehillim*, 2:11): even at times of "trembling" there is also an "exultant joy."

ALL YOUR ACTIONS FOR THE SAKE OF HEAVEN

The fulfillment of the words of the Sages, ". . . and all your actions should be for the sake of Heaven," is a real possibility only when the conversation that we take part in, and the study that we apply ourselves to, is informed by, and permeated with, the fear of Heaven.

THE DESIRE FOR *GAN EDEN*

In days gone by, in the courtyard and the thoroughfare—wherever Jews gathered together—the fear of Heaven, so deeply-rooted in their minds, was the sentiment that united them. Even among the simple and the unlettered of both sexes, one never failed to meet with a child-like fear of punishment, the fear of *gehinnom* and the infinite gradations of punishment reserved for the sinner; and, conversely, a yearning for the

the sinner; and, conversely, a yearning for the reward of *gan eden*—the world-to-come.

True, *Chasidus* explains the concepts of reward and punishment from a far loftier viewpoint, requiring us, concomitantly, to attain to higher and higher levels of the fear of Heaven. But all this has as its purpose, not to replace, but to augment, the fear of Heaven and the fear of punishment (in the literal sense), since this precisely is the purpose of *Chasidus*: to add and not, Heaven forbid, to subtract. This, it cannot be disputed, is the very minimum an individual must possess. For educators the task must be to instil these profound concepts in the hearts and minds of the students.

Alas, even the *concept* of fear seems to have no place in today's world. For this reason, we who know what the world does not, must double and redouble our efforts to strengthen *yirat shamayim*—both in concept and in practice.

THE RESPONSIBILITY OF THE EDUCATOR

The education of children brings with it awesome responsibilities—yet there are those who think it a distraction from the "real business of living."

If a student graduating from a Yeshiva school does not in his behavior give evidence of the fear of Heaven, his mother cannot be faulted for questioning the wisdom of having sent him to such a school in the first place. She might perhaps have done better— her thinking will go—if she had sent her child to a state school. As for Torah education—a private tutor, hired for so many hours a week, would have met the need.

And things will go from bad to worse—this you can depend on—when the mother shares her disenchantment with her neighbor, as a result of which being that neither of them will have the slightest interest in sending any more of their children to a Yeshivah school.

A LIVING EXAMPLE

Yirat shamayim is a fundamental principle in Jewish education. It cannot be transmitted successfully unless it permeates the conduct of the teachers themselves—living examples able to inspire their students to follow in their path.

CHAPTER 16
FAITH

STRENGTHENING FAITH

The situation in the Jewish world at large: the plague of immodesty spreading unchecked; estrangement from and ignorance of the ways of the past; the weakening of family ties—all this calls for a strengthening of faith in every segment of the population, children, youth, adults. We must respond to the crises facing us on so many fronts by a consolidation of our forces, in order to shore up and bolster faith in G-d, in the Torah, in our Sages and in our *tzaddikim*.

What is the nature of this faith and trust? In the words of Rashi, (*B'shalach*, 15:20): "The righteous women of the generation had complete faith that G-d would work miracles for them, and brought timbrels with them when they left Egypt."

Faith must penetrate deep within the soul; it must be rooted and embedded, steadfast and immovable. Faith at the level of question and answer, of a facility with words—as when, being tested on matters of faith and "having all the answers," we seem invincible—is not enough. For such faith is a house of cards, it is hollow, without substance.

To arrive at true faith, there must be total immersion in the subject, a thorough investigation of all that faith entails. Then the topic will penetrate deep into the mental life of the student, filling his or her thoughts, an endless process of discovery.

Akin to the shot that a doctor gives to his patient, to fight infection and strengthen resistance to disease, so also is there a spiritual "shot" that the educator must give to the student, to help him or her withstand and overpower whatever is hostile to faith—that being the world in which we find ourselves, where the forces of irreligion are on the march, and on the ascendant.

BELIEVING AND NOT BELIEVING

The Torah states that Noach was righteous and without stain. Nevertheless, as our Sages point out, (Rashi, *Noach*, 7:7), "He believed and did not believe." Even after one hundred and twenty years of uninterrupted labor: constructing the ark and publicizing the nature of the approaching Flood, he *still* wavered—"did not believe." Nevertheless, in spite of this subtle dichotomy—the condition of believing and not believing—the Torah states that he remained righteous and without stain.

The lesson that we draw from this is simply that all of us, without exception, and whatever our level, need constantly to strengthen our faith.

FORTIFYING FAITH

Tell the students stories of self-sacrifice—*mesirat nefesh*—in earlier generations: Chana and her seven sons, for example; stories from the time of the Inquisition; incidents in the lives of the "Cantonists." Such stories inspire faith.

At a more conceptual level, the chapter, "*Shaar HaBechinah*," in the book "*Chovot Halevavot*" (Rabbenu Yonah) can be used to illuminate faith-related issues. The simple faith that this material is capable of instilling can then be built upon by examining the subject through the prism of Chasidic teachings.

THE THIRTEEN PRINCIPLES

For reasons that are self-evident, every student must know the Thirteen Principles of Faith of Maimonides.

CHAPTER 17
GOOD
CHARACTER TRAITS

EDUCATING FOR GOOD CHARACTER TRAITS

Educational institutions must place a special emphasis on the *mitzvot* that deal with social relations of all kinds. They must seek to educate the heart of the student—helping him or her to develop the entire range of moral qualities, while avoiding a too-narrow emphasis on intellectual achievement. The Rebbe, Rabbi Yosef Yitzchak, once thundered at a farbrengen: "What is *Chasidus* without good *middot!*"

Study, discussion, guidance, contacts of all kinds—no alternative must be neglected in our effort to mould the character of the student along the right lines.

The grounding in good *middot* will make a significant contribution to the education of the child, the benefits radiating in all directions, bringing an increase of filial piety, consideration for others, and so on.

There is a general misconception that what belongs to the sphere of human relations is one thing, and what belongs to the sphere of "the fear of Heaven"—*yirat shamayim*—another. When we look into the *Shulchan Aruch*, however, we see that the former is a fundamental concern of Judaism, and that every Jew has an obligation to acquire good *middot*, no different, in essence, from the obligation to imitate the attributes of the Creator.

Through a comprehensive study of these laws, and taking the Rambam's *Hilchot De'ot* as our starting-point, we must combat and dispel this ignorance. Only by throwing *all* our resources at the problem can we hope to enlighten the unenlightened and bring our world to the level of virtuous action.

A further measure of the importance of the task is the fact that even Yom Kippur does not atone for the wrongs that we do our fellow-Jew, until and unless we seek his or her forgiveness—no other proof is needed of the urgency that we must bring to these matters.

In *parshat Kedoshim* reference is made to many fundamental good *middot*, and educators should make this *parsha* the focus of a generous amount of class discussion.

IMPARTING GOOD *MIDDOT*

The Rebbe, Rabbi Yosef Yitzchak, was insistent on this point, that in everything that we study we should find an object lesson for our daily lives.

The teacher must look upon everything that he or she teaches the child, the *parshat ha-shavuah*, for example, and of course the stories of our Sages, as a model for daily conduct and a spur to the acquisition of good character traits. A lesson devoted to the practical details of *halacha* is the ideal medium for this. It is a good idea to set aside part of the lesson—either at the beginning or the end—for free and informal conversation with the students and, by bringing out into the open, (sympathetically and discreetly), some problem that has recently emerged, to help the students tackle it in an adult manner. The problem should be addressed, not in a spirit of reproach, but in a way that leaves the student whose actions the discussion pertains to, in no uncertainty as to its relevance to his own "case."

THE INNER DIMENSION OF LEARNING

We must implant in the student the conviction that in everything that he is learning there is something of direct relevance to him, something that "speaks to him." We must pay attention not only to the quantity of the material learned, but also to the quality of the learning itself—to focus upon those elements of the subject that address the student, and the student's situation, in the most intimate manner.

Herein lies another great educational principle—developing the student's powers of introspection, that he may discover his shortcomings and resolve to perfect himself.

FORBEARANCE

We must let the children know how important it is to be forbearing, and give them the help they need to acquire this trait.

In the words of our Sages (*Yoma*, 23a), "Those who act with forbearance have all their sins forgiven." If this is so, when troubles come upon him, and "There are no troubles without wrongdoing and sin (as their root cause)" (*Shabbat*, 55a), it is in his power to free himself of them through this very forbearance—by means of which he is forgiven for all his own misdeeds.

LOVING-KINDNESS

The school should be the kind of place in which it comes naturally to the students to help each other in their learning, interest themselves in each other's welfare and, above all, give each other whatever practical help they can.

Similarly, students should be encouraged to do acts of loving-kindness on their own initiative, helping the blind, the elderly, visiting institutions that care for the elderly—aiding them, cheering them up, and so on.

SHOWING THE WORLD A CHEERFUL FACE

We must impress upon the students the importance of cheerfulness and of treating each other in a manner that befits young adults.

By the same token, when we hand something to the poor, it is important to do it graciously and with a smiling face—"(and) one should speak comforting words to him,"*(Bava Batra,* 9b).

Our Sages require this of us even in the act of honoring our mother and father, *(Kiddushin,* end of 31a), "There is the son that will set the tastiest bird before his father and vex him to death, and the son that will grind him his meal with his bare hands, yet cause him to taste of the life to come."

When we do a good deed for another person, it must be done out of fellow-feeling, out of a concern that the recipient should feel there are others who care for him and only desire what is best for him.

NOT TO VEX THE SPIRIT OF ANOTHER

In the Torah, *(B'har,* 25:17), it is stated: "Do not afflict one another." The verse is referring to the type of oppression practiced by the tongue. In other words, we are forbidden to vex or distress a fellow-Jew even through speech, *(Kitzur Shulchan Aruch,* 63:1). The Torah prohibits this no less than it prohibits the eating of swine, yet the students, in general, do not demonstrate awareness of the fact. Therefore, we must fill this gap in their knowledge and leave them in no doubt that it is forbidden to distress a friend—and one's parents, (whom there is also the mitzvah to honor), how much more so!

We must teach them the importance of understanding and considering the feelings of others, and of addressing them in the proper manner—saying what has to be said without causing pain or embarrassment, and leaving the other party satisfied that his or her point of view has been given due consideration, even if rejected.

By being taught, as a first step, to respect the feelings of others, the child is set firmly on the path to fulfilling the mitzvah of loving its fellow-Jew.

When what animates us most is consideration for others, this may also function as an antidote to the poison of domestic strife. Only let him internalize the above-mentioned *issur* and there is every prospect that, when he marries and builds a kosher home, he will never become the type who makes the life of his wife and his children an unrelieved misery.

It should be pointed out in this connection that sometimes the causing of pain or distress can be a positive thing, for example, the punishment given by a teacher who genuinely desires the good of the student; or the pain caused by a doctor in the course of treating sickness or injury; or by a *shochet* (slaughterer), who elevates the animal and makes it fit for consumption.

ANGER

"Anger is an evil trait and it is better for a person to keep away from it entirely, (and this in spite of the fact that, generally speaking, a person should choose the middle way). *Chazal* also hold that indulging in anger is tantamount to idol-worship," (*Kitzur Shulchan Aruch*, 29:4).

The children should be told stories about Tannaim and Amoraim who, no matter how much they were provoked, or taunted, held themselves back and silently endured.

I would also point out that through the telling of a story about *Chazal* the teacher is able at times to move a student so profoundly as to affect the course of his or her later development.

Apropos, we generally underestimate the stimulus that the teacher's telling of a delightful story can provide to the student, in terms of motivation and interest. Beyond the immediate impact, it is most likely that he will recall its content even many years later when again it will work its magic on him.

To Every Dispute, a Happy Conclusion

When two men take hold, (i.e., dispute possession), of a *tallit*, (this being a paradigm for cases of conflicting claims), each of the claimants is entitled to plead his case, and each has a basis for his claim in the laws of the Torah. However, after their case is settled in the *bet din*, the two must put their differences behind them and only be on good terms thereafter. And the same applies to children—when words are traded and fists fly. After the principal or the teacher has mediated between them, they must be reconciled, letting bygones be bygones. This is an attribute we dearly wish our students to possess.

Controversy

Everything that causes division and enmity must be torn up by the roots. Even though no two views will ever be identical, and in the interests of truth each must give voice to what he believes, Heaven forbid that this should lead to division or conflict.

On the contrary, if justice is to be served we *must* let the other man have his say, even if our respective views are totally opposed, for only in this way is it possible to arrive at a truthful conclusion. Having achieved this, we either adopt one of the views, or agree to a compromise, containing elements of both.

We have to teach the children, as soon as they are old enough to understand, that they must always heed the opinions and the feelings of the other person; then, even in their old age, this habit will not desert them.

For example, when a child who is in dispute, or has a quarrel, with his friend, comes to plead his cause before the teacher, the latter must listen with all seriousness, (for to the child this is a very serious matter)—in the same manner that, when an halachic inquiry is presented to him, the adjudicating rabbi will take in all the details and delve into the matter most carefully. From such an example the child will understand the necessity of giving due weight to the other person's opinion, so that in *adult* life such a principle will not be the least alien to his thinking.

Furthermore, when the child sees that he has the teacher's attention and is being treated like a grown-up, he will be that much more amenable to the teacher's counsel, allowing himself to be reconciled with his friend and acquiring in the process a fondness for the ways of peace-making.

If our educational institutions were to devote more time to instruction in the art of conflict resolution, we might see a good deal less conflict among adults, than that which we unfortunately do see today.

THE DISGRUNTLED STUDENT

The disgruntled student—we have all met him, for he is to be found in every school: the student who cannot open his mouth unless it is to gripe, about the school, his friends, his surroundings, etc. This is a shameful trait and we must give it short shrift whenever we meet with it, supplanting it, (by dint of persistence), with the love of one's fellow-Jew, trust in G-d, harmony and truthfulness.

LIVING EXAMPLE

We cannot expect our students to take the idea of perfecting oneself seriously unless they see "their betters" making strenuous efforts to improve their own *middot*, (by addressing each other, and their students, politely, refraining from *loshon hora*, valuing the student's time, and so on).

A TWO-PRONGED THRUST

Medical science works in two overlapping spheres—the strengthening and immunization of the healthy, and the cure and rehabilitation of the sick. So it is with *chinuch*: our task is to strengthen and consolidate the good traits that the student already possesses, and eradicate the undesirable ones.

A PRACTICAL SUGGESTION

Arrange a series of talks on the subject of good *middot*, attitudes, and so on, dividing them up in such a way that one particular topic will be covered over the course of several days, supported by all kinds of examples, supplementary material, and so on. This will bring the topic home to the students in a more forceful manner and they will be more likely to retain it.

CHAPTER 18
LOVE OF
ONE'S FELLOW-JEW

"THE BOTTOM LINE"

The Rebbe appealed consistently for the strengthening and invigorating of the mitzvah of *"Ahavat Yisrael"*—the love of one's fellow-Jew.

We must strive at least to reach the minimal level in this mitzvah, whose nature can best be gauged from the words of our Sages concerning Hillel, (*Shabbat*, 31a): when a convert came to him with the request to teach him Torah "on one foot"—to convey its essence to him while sparing him the details—he replied: "What is hateful to you do not do unto your friend." Hillel did not present him with the obverse, or positive, obligation, that of loving one's fellow-Jew, for had he done so, the convert might have launched into a whole series of questions—what is the measure of this love, how far are we to take it, where exactly does it apply, and how? (and, indeed, there is no end to the details). Rather he framed his answer negatively, "what is hateful to you *do not do* unto others," and all is in this negative, for where one is in doubt, the answer is "No, you are not to inflict this upon the other person!"

THAT WHICH IS HATEFUL TO YOU

We must bring out in our students the latent capacity to love one's fellow-Jew, not just in theory but in actuality. The words of Hillel, "What is hateful to you, etc." must be their guiding light: in everything that they undertake, to consider how they would wish to be treated by others, and to apply those very same standards—a rigorous dialectic—in their conduct towards them.

A HEARTFELT LOVE

Ahavat Yisrael is not simply a matter of what one does or does not do, it is rather a spontaneous and direct outpouring of the heart. This is how things once were—the love for a fellow Jew welled up in the heart, was something palpable.

AN UNCONDITIONAL LOVE

We must get the children to understand, that when Shimon does something to harm Reuven, and Reuven takes Shimon to a *din* Torah, and the verdict goes against Shimon—Reuven is not thereby exempted from the duty and the mitzvah to love every Jew, Shimon included. This holds true even if Shimon acted wickedly, for he must surmount this obstacle and love him not a jot less—in this respect it is no different from any other mitzvah: when there is some obstacle to its fulfillment, we try to surmount it, and fulfill the mitzvah.

In such a case, where one is the innocent victim of a wrong, he must draw upon a love whose source lies deeper still, a love which is unconditional, which even the acts of others have no power to affect. So much so that if Shimon has sunk, spiritually speaking, to such a level, the greater is the obligation to have pity on him and help him mend his ways. And if Providence willed that he should harm Reuven, this is a sure sign that it is

Reuven himself who must be the prime mover in helping him achieve this.

All of which runs counter to the popular but misguided view that if someone treats you badly, you can "dish out" the same treatment to him.

There is a further point to consider. As is explained in *Tanya*, (*Igeret Hakodesh*, 25), "the fact that he sustained a loss is the result of a Heavenly decree"; we see, therefore, that in essence his loss was pre-existent, for it was decreed from Above, save that it was Shimon who chose, or was chosen, to execute this decree.

It might well be that Shimon acted inadvertently, or was unaware that he was inflicting so grievous a loss. However, since Reuven was the injured party, it behooves him to help Shimon do *teshuvah* and become a better person. When Reuven rises to the challenge and relates to Shimon in this way, it shows that, in the very act of causing him a loss, Reuven was purely and simply the instrument of the Divine plan, as revealed in the workings of Providence.

THE LOVE OF OUR FELLOW-JEW AND JEWISH UNITY

The Rebbe called for and demanded, not only *Ahavat Yisrael*, but *Achdut Yisrael*—Jewish unity.

No doubt the children have asked their teachers to explain the differences between these two concepts.

The answer is: *Ahavat Yisrael* implies: I love the other person—although there still remain two distinct entities, Myself and the Other, existing in all their separateness, and with all the possibilities of conflict that this separateness contains.

Hence, "You shall love your neighbor as *yourself*," (*Kedoshim*, 19:18), where the point and the emphasis are on "as yourself"—just as you fight for your place in the sun, so you should recog-

ust as you fight for your place in the sun, so you should recognize and make allowance for the strivings of your neighbor—they are in essence identical to your own.

The body comprises 248 limbs and 365 sinews. Only when they are all linked and bound together is man called Man, and while, theoretically, G-d could have made man in the form of a "kit," with all his parts available for use as and when required, He clearly chose not to do so, integrating them, instead, into that complex unity which is the pinnacle of Creation. The unity of his bodily parts becomes a paradigm for the social and spiritual interrelations of the Jew with his fellow-Jews and helps us to understand the concept of:

Achdut Yisrael—the unity of the Jewish people—which, in contrast to *Ahavat Yisrael*, describes a condition in which Self and Other are identical, there no longer being a "first person" and a "second person," (an I and a Thou). Rather, we are all joined together, literally, like the limbs of one organism. Jewish unity is an innate property of the Jewish soul, (as explained in *Tanya*, chap. 32), and from the standpoint of the soul, this oneness, this unity, is not a figure of speech, but reality pure and simple.

LIKE BROTHERS, LITERALLY

Among chasidim, love, brotherhood and friendship were part of the natural order. The chasidim were not just like one family, but like brothers, in everything but name. This had always been the core of *Chasidus*, the glue that held that world together. What we have nowadays, however, is only a pale reflection of that reality. This is something that needs to be candidly discussed with all age groups and levels of understanding.

THE LOVE OF OUR FELLOW-JEW AND THE LOVE OF G-D

Whenever, out of feelings of *ahavat Yisrael*, we do a good deed for a fellow Jew, this is no less an expression of "*ahavat Hashem*,"—the love of G-d. Which is only what one would expect, since one cannot love the father without benefiting the son. Conversely, a love for the father is inherent in any act of kindness to the son. Thus, the love is reinforced for both father and son.

PEACE

Discuss *shalom*—peace, with the children. Time and time again we ask for peace: we begin our prayers with the words, "I hereby undertake to fulfil the commandment to love my fellow-Jew as myself"; "grant peace," and more. Challenge the children to make a list of the number of times the word "peace" is mentioned in our prayers.

CHAPTER 19
PRINCIPLES OF
CONDUCT AND DECORUM

CIVILITY AND ETIQUETTE

When we turn our attention to the related subjects of etiquette and the cultivation of social graces, we find that ignorance, and the uncouthness that results, is the rule. Even schools that should know better make little or no provision for the study of the relevant *halachot*.

We educators must not neglect to give the children a proper grounding in these concepts: to show respect to the elderly, for example, through performing the mitzvah of "(You shall) rise before the elderly," (*Kedoshim*, 19:32), on bus and train especially, but wherever the opportunity presents itself. This is by no means a trivial point. As the Rambam emphasizes, (*Hilchot De'ot*, 5:1), we recognize the wise by everything they do: not only by their actions, but by the way they speak, the way they eat and the way they drink—in a word, by their manners. All this is a fundamental principle in education.

In various editions of the *Chumash Chok L'Yisrael*, are printed the *Orchot Chaim* of the Rosh, and *Archei Yisrael*, both of which provide us with practical definitions of civility and decorous behavior.

It is vital to restore this subject to its rightful place in the curriculum, and thence to the minds and hearts of the students. Admittedly, there is a temptation to downplay it because it only has to do with "externals," but—externals act upon the inner person and upon all that a person does, and, beyond this, help to shape and refine our moral being.

If we will only attend to this, the character and temperament of our students will be transformed before our eyes, bringing with it a *kiddush Hashem*—a sanctification of the name of G-d—causing the world to sit up and take notice, and exclaim "See, how noble are their ways when we compare them to. . . ."

CLEANLINESS

Cleanliness is a must in education. Of course, we all have an obligation not to go unwashed and unkempt, as taught in the *Mishnah*, (*Sotah*, chap. 9, *mishnah* 15) "Cleanliness brings one to a state of purity." Be it noted that the beginning of the *Shulchan Aruch*, which deals with the first activities of the day, is much occupied with matters of cleanliness, (the washing of the hands, examining oneself before prayer, washing out one's mouth, and so on).

The children must be taught these *halachot* and trained to be fastidious with regard to cleanliness of person, (a pre-requisite for prayer), and of dress, (shoes polished, shirts immaculate) down to the last detail.

We therefore expect every student to maintain a high level of personal cleanliness, including—it goes without saying—the regular cutting and cleaning of the nails, (which can affect the validity of the washing of the hands).

Both in their person and in their dress they should look well groomed and make a pleasing impression.

Cleanliness has its own part to play in the development of character. Similarly, it can have a positive effect on others, reflecting favorably on the school. The reverse is also possible, since an outsider, catching sight of students who look ill-clad or unwashed will have second thoughts about sending his or her child to a school that appears to disregard such a state of affairs.

GARMENTS OF THE BODY, GARMENTS OF THE SOUL

"You are children to the L-ord your G-d, form not factions, neither make a bald spot between your eyes," (*R'eh*, 14:1). Since the Children of Israel are children of the Holy One—and are also called "the children of kings," (*Shabbat*, 67a), and even "kings," (*Berachot*, 9b)—it is only to be expected that their physical appearance be regal. Hence, they are forbidden to make incisions or disfigure themselves in any other way, (as explained by Rashi, commenting on that verse—you are children of G-d, and you should look regal). It is self-evident, then, that the garments that clothe such a body must contribute to that effect.

Cleanliness in the garments of the body can lead to cleanliness in the "garments" of the soul, which are thought, speech and action. A Jew is always in the presence of the King, "and Hashem stands over him and watches him, examining both mind and heart, assessing the righteousness of his acts," (*Tanya*, chap. 41). A person must strive, therefore, for a spiritual garment, as befits one who stands before the King. His thoughts must be pure and unsullied; his speech seemly and refined—and as for his actions, they must *a fortiori* exhibit these qualities.

We must drum these principles into the students from their earliest years, and every teacher, (similarly, every one occupying a communal position, be he rabbi, *gabbai* or fund-raiser), must strive to be a living embodiment of them.

LAWS OF MEAL-TIMES

In order to ensure an habitual atmosphere of calm, restraint and good manners, every aspect of mealtimes should come under strict supervision, The good habits the students acquire at such times will stay with them for the rest of their lives.

We have an obligation to teach the students table manners, namely, the laws that govern meal taking, as elaborated in the *Shulchan Aruch*. *Hilchot De'ot* of the Rambam should also be consulted in this context, prescribing as it does the proper way for a Jew to eat, drink, and stroll in public—as recommended by the Rebbe on many occasions.

KIDDUSH HASHEM—SANCTIFYING G-D'S NAME

The students must have a proper conception of *kiddush Hashem*, as well as of its antithesis. The idea is not in essence that one must give up one's life for *kiddush Hashem*. Clean fingernails, spotless clothes, polished shoes, giving up one's seat on the bus to an elderly person—all these are elements of *kiddush Hashem*.

Proper behavior is in itself the fulfillment of a positive mitzvah of the Torah, the mitzvah of *kiddush Hashem*, and so with the converse, G-d forbid.

So viewed, no detail of one's behavior is without significance, even the simple acts of walking in the street, eating and drinking, and so on. When good behavior attracts the attention of the passer-by and he is impressed by what he sees, he thinks to himself: this is how the G-d-fearing behave, and is even motivated to be more G-d-fearing himself—this truly is *kiddush Hashem*! And the converse—his seeing something that makes his gorge rise—is *chillul Hashem*.

CHAPTER 20
SPEECH

REFINEMENT IN SPEECH

The students need to understand that there is much more to the idea of acceptable speech than the mere avoidance of the forbidden—as profanity, gutter language, and the like. In effect, they must aim to cultivate a certain style, a style of speech without abrasiveness, discreet, tactful and refined, (even though refinement of speech is no guarantee of refinement of soul).

As our Sages have taught, (*Pesachim*, 3a), "Scripture spoke in a roundabout way and added eight letters rather than utter a shameful thing," (by using the circumlocution, "which were not clean" rather than the term "unclean"—in Hebrew, *tameh*, the force of which is not conveyed by the English word "unclean").

Chasidus explains that although the care that we take to moderate our speech is an aspect of our social relations, hence of the "external world," it (this care) nonetheless has a direct effect upon our inner lives, for the simple reason that the garment—in this case, the garment of speech—"acts upon the wearer."

Here too, we can learn from the conduct of the Rebbe, who took great care whenever he spoke to avoid the slightest suspicion of impropriety.

THE VOICE IS THE VOICE OF YAAKOV

In the passage where he gives his blessing to Yaakov his son, Yitzchak utters the words, "The voice is the voice of Yaakov,"

(*Toldot*, 27:22), and Rashi explains that it was the characteristic refinement of his voice that Yitzchak recognized: "for he (Yaakov) spoke in a deferential manner," (additionally, that the name of Heaven was constantly on his lips, see Rashi's comment on verse 21).

The point this passage is making is that there was no appreciable difference between the voices of Yaakov and Eisav. Had that been the case, Yitzchak would have recognized Yaakov by his voice alone, rather than by the way he expressed himself. As it is, we have to conclude that their voices were identical. The Rashbam on this passage notes: "Not surprisingly for twins, their voices sounded very similar."

Accordingly, what we derive from this passage is an object lesson in the importance of modest, dignified speech.

BOORISHNESS IN SPEECH

As mentioned above, (see beginning, Chap. 19), in various editions of *Chok L'Yisrael*, the *sefer Orchot Chaim* of the *Rosh* and other works of a similar nature have been incorporated. These provide models of the civilized behavior and simple good manners that should be the norm in daily life. For example: "Do not talk like a boor," that is: one should speak in measured tones, without drawing attention to oneself, and not with a loud voice, like an uncouth person." When a child reared along these lines reaches manhood, he will have the good sense not to "bawl out" his own children, (something which can harm them psychologically and therefore affect their ability to learn), nor shake the rafters with his outbursts, in this way protecting the delicate bloom of domestic peace.

(Be it noted: most problems that develop between husband and wife are attributable to a want of refinement in speech and *middot*).

I think it would be a commendable idea to publish an anthology of sayings culled from *Orchot Chaim*, dealing with such topics as discretion and delicacy of speech. Some of this could be perhaps be copied down in class and memorized.

PROFANITIES, CURSES AND OATHS

We must help our students fulfill the commandment not to let an unclean word or unclean thought cross one's lips. They are required to shun the use of profanities and curses, (in any shape or form), even the frivolous oaths that are common currency among students.

It goes without saying that, for maximum effectiveness, every school will need to use its own ingenuity in finding the best way to drive these points home.

TRUTH

Truth is not monolithic, nor is it a blunt instrument. Not always are we called upon to speak the whole truth. In fact, there are times when the truth is best left unsaid, and there are matters best concealed from view. However, falsehood—the telling of lies—is to be condemned unequivocally, for it is an abomination. We must convey with all the force at our disposal that none of us has any other choice than to be truthful and honest—to be an "*ish emet*," a person of integrity, someone whose word is his bond.

This principle must be so firmly established in the student's heart that even in the privacy of his own thoughts he will acknowledge the truth, and in the ordinary way of speech will never stoop to falsehood. As a result, people will take him at his word, for he is an "*ish emet*," a person of integrity, one in whom we can place our trust.

DISTANCE YOURSELF FROM FALSEHOOD

It is known that the Alter Rebbe insisted upon the truth and but for this would have had many more chasidim, (*Hayom Yom*, 10th Menachem Av). Nevertheless, even if one cannot attain to the level of truthfulness, he can at least distance himself from falsehood, "Keep thee far from a false matter," (*Mishpatim*, 23:6), and this will help him steer clear of many a pitfall. One's urge to tell the truth should be so great as to cause him to shrink from committing certain acts, knowing full well that if he did so, he could not, under questioning, bring himself to deny the fact. However, in the fullness of time he will arrive at a genuine feeling for the truth, (as opposed to intellectual acceptance and the fear of detection, alone).

TEN VARIETIES OF *LASHON HARA*—GOSSIP

In *Shaarei Teshuva* of Rabbenu Yona, (Third Gate), there is a lengthy discussion of those aspects of human relations that call for delicacy and thoughtfulness but which, in the course of daily affairs, tend to be lost sight of or ignored.

Reference is made in that section, *inter alia*, to ten types of *lashon hara*—the ways in which one harms others through the action of the tongue.

(In this section he also focuses on the "malcontent," the aggrieved individual who is forever dwelling on the wrongs done to him. This is a person whose grievances may indeed be justified, but whether this is the case or not, he has made a full-time occupation out of being as full of grievances as a pomegranate of seeds).

"REMEMBER . . . MIRIAM"

An educator must search tirelessly for ways to help and spur the child toward greater control of its gift of speech. Of particular relevance in this context is the fifth of the "Six Remembrances" that we recite every day: "Remember what the L-rd your G-d did to Miriam on the way when you left Egypt."

Clearly Miriam did not wish to malign her brother Moshe— quite the contrary, she had risked her life to save his, and her intentions were nothing if not honorable. Of whom are we speaking? Of Miriam the Prophetess! Of she who, even after she said what she said about Moshe, forfeited not one iota of her greatness. Of Miriam, whom the people honored with one voice and whose every word they revered. And yet, when she fell from grace by uttering a forbidden thing, her punishment was of such severity that we make mention of it every single day. From this circumstance we may learn, *a fortiori*, how to regard prohibited speech—the stages by which we are brought first to speak, then to gossip, about another human being until, finally, we make our slanderous or otherwise injurious remarks.

In Rashi's words, (*B'haalotecha*, 12:1), "Just as Miriam was punished, though she intended no dishonor, how much more so (is punishment warranted) when one intentionally casts a slur on one's fellow."

PRACTICAL ADVICE

What I recommend is the following: a series of talks devoted to speech in all its guises. Every day the teacher should introduce the children to a different aspect on the subject, until they arrive at a full appreciation of the complex ways in which speech affects their lives and their well being.

The following scheme may serve as a model for this topic:

There are three categories: permitted speech, empty talk, forbidden speech. The category of the permitted also embraces the manner of speaking, which may be refined or crude. Similarly, we find speech that is eloquent and graceful, speech that inspires, speech that consoles and speech that delights. At the opposite extreme, we find lying and deceit, slander, vulgarity, and so on, in all of which one puts to destructive use the gift of speech given by G-d to Man alone, (see in this connection the commentary of the Rambam to *Avot*, 1:17).

And—as is known—life and death are in the power of the tongue.

In conclusion, there is speech that brings (us) to sanctification of G-d's name: when strangers hear the students speaking pleasantly and are suitably impressed, this reflects well on the institution that has left its mark on them, winning plaudits for all the fine work it is doing.

We must explore this theme in all its manifestations, until lying and deceit, gossip and slander, with all their base progeny, arouse nothing but repulsion and disgust in the students; until, conversely, their one desire will be to use the faculty of speech for what is worthy only, as it is said, (*V'etchanan*, 6:7): "And you shall speak of them."

CHAPTER 21
DISCIPLINING
ONE'S THOUGHTS

EDUCATING FOR THOUGHT

Educators conventionally focus on speech and action, treating the topic of thought as if it were only of marginal importance. However, this approach is a mistaken one; it is, in fact, crucially important to impart an understanding of thought, and the machinery of thought, and of the dangers that its workings hold for us.

In practice, everyone is careful not to commit a forbidden act and not to hold back from performing a positive one—and none of us would dream of taking as our authority anything but the words of the Torah—which is precisely the message we pass on to our students. We are also wary of forbidden speech, (though to a much lesser extent, and we need to wake up to this fact). However, we do not do enough to stress the fact that all of us are responsible for the thoughts and meditations of our hearts.

We treat action, then, with the seriousness it deserves, speech less so. *Thought*, however, languishes in obscurity. Indeed, I have yet to find the subject taken up anywhere; the educational world at large seems to feel no particular obligation to place it on the agenda or to make students aware of its seriousness.

HOLY THOUGHTS

A child must be brought up to be sensitive to the concept of purity of thought, and to the formative role that thought plays in its life; to the need to concentrate its thoughts and imagination on words of Torah and all that falls within the sphere of Torah. Furthermore, it has to acquire this knowledge in early childhood, for it is a fundamental part of education.

When the world of thought is reclaimed for holiness, speech and action yield without a struggle. On the other hand, a head where thought runs free is a place of ruin, demons gather there! For the educator has no difficulty judging the degree to which the child controls his speech and his behavior—but what goes on inside his head, where all is obscure, of this he has no inkling!

When teacher, parent and child unite in their recognition of the importance of disciplining and keeping thought on a tight rein—they will all stand firm against anything which seeks to undermine that discipline, such as TV and films, and the like.

DO NOT FOLLOW

We must sharpen awareness of the important negative commandment, "You shall not follow after your eyes and after your heart," (*Sh'lach*, 15:39), and of the urgency of keeping one's thoughts in line. When the student really comes to know and understand this commandment, he will automatically be on guard against anything capable of engendering improper thoughts, will not let his eyes wander hither and thither, and so forth.

SEVERAL KINDS OF FORBIDDEN THOUGHT

What calls for such curbs and restraints? Among other things, even the idea of doing something forbidden, such as eating "*treifah*," and similar abominations. And the same applies, logically enough, to any negative thoughts and feelings that we find ourselves harboring towards another, (see *Tanya, Igeret Hakodesh*, end of chapter 22).

WHAT THOUGHT CAN ACCOMPLISH

In general, we do not recognize that we are totally responsible for our own thoughts—hence, we must stress the miraculous power of positive thinking, the power that it has to change a person, as is brought out in *Chasidus* in connection with "thinking *Chasidus*," (the transformation that can be wrought in a person through the chasidic practice of calm and balanced reflection). But we must also stress the converse. Those who study *Chasidus* already have a conception of the lofty potential of thought and the scope of its influence, and know how careful we must be to keep our thoughts within a framework and to sift their content.

"Thought makes a difference," (see *Likkutei Dibburim*, Vol. 1, p. 2), both for benefactor and for beneficiary, and ultimately has much greater repercussions than speech or action.

Thought acts upon the soul. Sometimes a thought leaves a deeper impression than either speech or action, and it is difficult to free oneself of it, so that it ends by leading us down a dangerous path.

EXTRA CARE

More so than with speech and action, the silent machinery of thought demands the closest supervision if its workings are not to overwhelm us. There are three reasons for this:

First, in the very nature of things, people do not suspect that they can be sinning with their thoughts; accordingly, they have no qualms about indulging in them, and never once did it occur to them that they have something to repent for.

Second, one's thoughts are never static, they are always in flux. Not to think at all is impossible, and even if we have the *illusion* that we are not thinking, in reality we are, for the stream of consciousness is never still. If, therefore, one does not "take command" and fill his mind with what is good and constructive, his thoughts will go their own merry way, snaring him in vanities, and worse.

Third, thought has a greater power to corrupt a person, precisely because of its subtlety, and its affinity to the soul.

HARD LABOR

Because true mastery of thought is difficult to attain, a greater expenditure of effort is required than many are willing to make. The student's thoughts, in particular, are in continual ferment, and all his actions and choices betray their influence. On the other hand, he does not at all foresee the consequences of his thinking, and this places him at constant risk.

GUARDING THE EYES PURIFIES ONE'S THOUGHTS

Because the things we gaze upon can make such a deep impression upon us, it is vitally important to exercise self-censorship in regard to all that we see. At times, even something seen long ago can rise without warning to the surface of the mind and work its mischief, so that only constant vigilance can help us achieve, and safeguard, purity of thought.

Upon whom else should it fall if not upon the parent and the educator to shield the child from seeing and being engrossed by those things which are harmful to it and which provide such fertile ground for the designs of the evil inclination.

To Saturate one's Thoughts with the Letters of Torah

A person has the ability to replace negative thoughts with their potent opposite. The Rebbes of Lubavitch have left us a rich legacy of teachings in this area; among them: the letters of Torah must be engraved in our minds and memory, as is explained in *Likkutei Torah, V'hadarta Pnei Zaken,* with the result that our thoughts will also be filled with them. When the student has committed a significant amount of Torah to memory, he can more effectively defend himself against the allure of sinful thoughts, for he has at his disposal the means to banish them from his mind—through the active review of all the Torah that he has memorized.

CHAPTER 22
MANAGING ONE'S TIME

THE PRECIOUSNESS OF TIME

The student must be taught to value and utilize, soundly and effectively, whatever time he has available to him and, by the same token, be shown how not to squander it. Not to be prodigal of one's time is of the greatest importance, and one must be strict with himself in this regard. If we succeed in endowing the student with a sense of the value of time, we lay down for him or her a foundation that will endure a lifetime.

Idleness and time wasting are the scourge of the modern age, one that has made inroads everywhere. Therefore, we must zealously root them out and plant diligence and persistence in their place.

WE CANNOT START TOO EARLY!

A child in kindergarten is not too young to be taught to value time: that it must sacrifice not even a moment to idleness, but use its time in productive ways. Even play-time and recess should be geared towards the development of the child, and everything should be organized around the idea of the benefit to be gained for him or her—for example, whatever games and sports they take part in, and the manner of their participation, can make a real difference in this respect.

PLAY-TIME

Play is a critical factor in a child's development. Here too, time should be put to the best use; the child's games should have educational value and not just be designed to keep it from making a nuisance of itself, for a vital phase in its development is taking place at this very time. So much so that if this time is not used to the best advantage, the child's development may well be delayed. The same set of factors affects us all, young or old—our time must be used sensibly and well.

NOT TO WASTE THE TIME OF OTHERS

The use or misuse of our time affects not only ourselves but also those around us, too. It is often found to be the case that when a student is wasting his own time his behavior is more than likely causing time-wasting in others.

Thus, being brought face-to-face with the effect on others of his actions, by being shown how his own time-wasting has spoiled things for them, can help develop in the student more civilized standards of behavior and a concept of mutuality.

ONE'S ALLOTTED SPAN

Everyone is allotted a certain number of years in accordance with their mission on this earth, in the words of the Psalmist, (139:16), ". . . the days also in which they are to be fashioned." It follows that we must not waste a single moment.

HOW TIME DIFFERS FROM THE REST OF CREATION

Time, along with the rest of Creation, was created for a definite purpose, although it can only fulfil this purpose through the medium and with the aid of man. However, in one respect time is not like the rest of Creation, since every other created thing has something that can step into its place—another representative of that class—so that a replacement is always on hand. Time, by contrast, cannot be replaced, and to fritter it away is to make a breach in Creation that can never be repaired.

TIME—LIFE

"Time is money," as Americans never tire of saying. For a Jew, however, time is *life*—the worth of our lives is measured in terms of the use we make of the time allotted to us. When a Jew lets a moment go by that could have been used for the service of G-d, a gap, as it were, opens up in his existence, for the Torah is "our life and the length of our days."

THE DAYS THAT LENGTHEN INTO YEARS

We must teach the student to live the day and every moment of the day to its fullest—so that each day's potential may be realized. A day is made up of hours and minutes. When is the day truly a day?—when all its hours leave a record of their passing; and when is an hour truly an hour?—when all the minutes that make it up are present and accounted for. Every moment, therefore, must be treasured. The oft-met Hebrew expression for long life, *arichat yamim v'shanim*, (literally, "length of days and years"), means that the days are "long," filled with the content that we have given them. When we treasure the moments, we treasure also the hours and the days. The years follow likewise.

TIME AND ORDER

When the student is orderly and disciplined in the use he makes of his time, so that he can be said to be using time properly—this leads to orderliness of thought, thence to orderliness in all of his undertakings, which ultimately lifts him to a higher level of existence, one where "the brain rules over the heart."

USING TIME TO OPTIMAL EFFECT

We must teach our students not only to use their time prudently, but also to use it optimally, in the most efficient and productive manner.

I recommend the setting-up of a special three-man task force, which should be invited to the school to draw up a blueprint for the most effective use of the school's study-time, in order to make these hours as productive as possible.

The same satisfaction would be afforded to adults, who would enjoy the services of a consultant directing and advising them how to make the most of their time.

ALL YOUR DEEDS FOR THE SAKE OF HEAVEN

Our Sages state, (*Avot*, 2:12), "And all your deeds shall be for the sake of Heaven." It is possible to explain this directive and duty in terms of the statement that "G-d made every single thing with a purpose," (*Bamidbar Rabba*, 8:18), and "Everything that G-d created in his world He only created for his own glory." (*Avot*, 6:11). Therefore, when we perform any act for the sake of Heaven, we consecrate the intention present at Creation, be it the intention concealed within the object with which we perform the act, be it that the man himself, by virtue of his act, consecrates the purpose of his *own* creation. Conversely, if we do not do this for the sake of Heaven, we introduce a blemish into the scheme of Creation.

The above is a topic of the deepest significance, and we must ensure that it makes the requisite impact.

The ideas dealt with here are also connected with the proper use of time. Time is also a creation, created for a particular purpose, namely, His blessed glory. Therefore, we must use it in the manner that best accords with this purpose, especially in connection with Torah study, which is an obligation binding upon every individual, and whose neglect is a dereliction of duty.

TIME (PROPERLY USED) IS A SHIELD FOR THOUGHT

Our task is to get the students to internalize this value. This will lead to discipline of the inner life, for—rest assured—idleness, lack of purpose and tedium can lead us down the path of destructive, impure thoughts, thoughts with no saving grace whatsoever. Therefore, we must strive to engage the student's mind constantly, in order not to leave him or her prey to any sort of distraction.

How often do we hear a child—or a grown-up, for that matter—saying,: "I'm bored, I've got nothing to do." But when that child realizes that nothing G-d made is without its purpose and that there is a reason for everything, and that, if he wants, he can use his mind for higher things, and that there is so much to do, so much to be done—then he will find himself bemoaning the scarcity of time, given all that he now proposes to accomplish. Surely *then* he will come to prize time and cherish it!

A LEAP YEAR

The Lubavitcher Rebbe, Rabbi Menachem M. Schneerson, wanted us to be aware that when the year is a full one, we must use the days in such a way that we fulfil the verse: "All that it was possible and necessary to do on each and every day, was done," (*Zohar Chadash*, Part 3, 94:2). During a leap year we are granted extra days, of which we must make good use, filling them with significant content; and it is certain that the strength to do so has also been granted us.

CHAPTER 23
JEWISH VALUES

ACCEPTING THE YOKE

"Acceptance of the yoke" is one of the cornerstones of education. It is incumbent on the student to accept the guidance of the educator out of a spirit of "*kabbalat ol*," and whether or not he understands what he is told is immaterial. The sixth Rebbe of Lubavitch, Rabbi Yosef Yitzchak Schneersohn, relates how he was taught that there are "no why's," and, as he puts it: "... when I was growing up, asking why was altogether out of the question; in fact, this word did not exist in our lexicon." Whereas, society has thrown off the yoke, inviting chaos in its place, and the trashing of values; and this spirit of anarchy has also infected Jewish circles and Jewish institutions. For we see how the student plays the intellectual, disputing every point with his teachers—and until we explain to his satisfaction why things must be so, he is not prepared to yield his ground—to the point where the teacher is forced to "strategize" in order to make his voice heard.

This state of affairs has sparked a number of crises in the area of *chinuch*, and institutions are bearing the brunt of it. When, on the other hand, there is *kabbalat ol*, there is *yirat shamayim*, and there is fear of the teacher, (analogous to the fear of Heaven). When there is no *kabbalat ol*, the fear in which the teacher should be held also suffers an eclipse. This results in lack of discipline, and the structure of the day is shaken to its foundations. When students will once again possess the authentic spirit of *kabbalat ol*, there will also, assuredly, be fewer discipline problems, a weakening of the impulse to rebel.

Yes, *Chasidus* explains, and concedes, that in addition to *kabbalat ol* there must also be understanding and comprehension, but the source and foundation of all is "acceptance of the yoke!"

Let me point out, in passing, that among the sayings of our Sages we find the expression, "a decree that the majority of the community is incapable of complying with (we do not impose upon them)," but the expression, "a decree that the majority of the community do not *desire*"—this we do not find.

We need to educate the broad masses and bring about a veritable change in the way they think, with regard to the importance of *kabbalat ol*.

"ITKAFIYA"—SELF-MASTERY

Teach the student to leave a little of the candy-bar unconsumed, that is, strive to develop in him or her the state of mind capable of such a "feat": the brain dominating the candy, and not *vice versa*—the candy dominating the brain.

SOUL-SEARCHING

We must accustom our students to engage in "stock-taking," always to be able to take stock of their actions and their behavior and to assess the type and degree of change necessary. There is the daily "stock-taking," before retiring, and the weekly "stock-taking," at the end of the week.

ORDERLINESS AND SYSTEM

We should expect of our students strict standards of orderliness, a virtue that will rain down blessings on them. To this end, the student must be given a clear picture of the important role that orderliness plays in every facet of his or her life—keeping his private space tidy; being punctual and constantly aware of the passing of time, enabling it to be utilized in the best possible way; tidiness of dress; an intelligent study-schedule, logical thinking, and so on.

"Order and system" are fundamental principals in *Chasidus*, as we learn from *Hayom Yom*, (7 Tammuz): that the Baal Shem Tov was orderly and systematic. The Maggid insisted upon order, and the Alter Rebbe taught the chasidim to be orderly. Indeed, the very bearing of a person testifies to the fact that he is orderly in all that he does, or to the exact opposite, as the case may be.

SELF-SACRIFICE

The children should have a clear picture of the self-sacrifice of the Jewish people during the two millennia of Exile.

They must also be given the opportunity to hear stories of every kind on the subject of *mesirat nefesh* for *kiddush Hashem*, (sanctification of G-d's name), and this must be made an integral part of the syllabus of studies. For example, Avraham Avinu in the fiery furnace, Chanania, Mishael and Azariya, the Ten Martyrs—among them Rabbi Akiva—cruelly slain by the Romans; and Chana and her seven sons.

This same theme runs through stories of the Inquisition, of the Cantonists, of the notorious decrees designed to force the Jewish people to abandon their religion, of the period of the Holocaust, and so on.

Wherever possible, exhibitions should be organized in commemoration of these historical events.

Today, of course, we are not in the position of having to give up our lives for *kiddush Hashem* in the literal sense, and we go so far as to pray to be spared such a fate, (Heaven protect us!). For all this, the simple truth is that we say in our recital of the *Shema* "and you shall love Him with all your heart and all your soul,"—meaning "even if he *takes* your soul," (*Berachot*, chap. 9, *mishnah* 5). Similarly, at the end of the *Ne'ilah* prayer, (on Yom Kippur), when we say "*Shema Yisrael*," everyone has to embrace the principle of self-sacrifice in actuality—the readiness to die to sanctify G-d's name. As we read in *Tanya*, (chap. 25), "The keeping of the Torah and its commandments depends upon the constant awareness that we may be called upon, in the name of the Torah, to make the ultimate sacrifice."

We must tap into the power of self-sacrifice that is latent in every Jew, the potency of the Jew, the "majesty of Yaakov." There was a time when Jews literally gave up their lives for sanctification of G-d's name; it follows, then, that they held themselves in a perpetual state of readiness to do so, and yet they did not make a great to-do about it—even their children acted in the same spirit. However, today, in the free world, one could be forgiven for thinking that this is a page in our history that no one is inclined to peruse any more.

Time must be devoted to this topic, to stories and explanations. When the child will thoroughly have absorbed the material, he or she will assuredly find the strength to face and to overcome every manner of hindrance and obstruction.

THE SELF-SACRIFICE OF CHILDREN

The children should be told stories and anecdotes, describing the self-sacrifice of children for the sanctification of G-d's name. This should be an inspiration for them to model their own behavior on the example of these heroic children and look for opportunities to sanctify the name of Heaven in their own lives.

The most appropriate time to present such material is the period known as *Bein Hametzarim* (the three-week period commemorating the first breach and the subsequent destruction of the Temple), save that care should be taken not to allow the dominant mood to be one of sadness and melancholy. Therefore, to counteract this, an element of joy should be added, to underscore the fact that one should take the act of *mesirat nefesh* and *kiddush Hashem* upon oneself, not in a spirit of gloom and resignation, but with joyfulness.

ASPIRING TO GREATER HEIGHTS

Truly things are not what they used to be. Once, you seldom met with the man or woman who was not consumed with the desire to make something of themselves; there was a will and a determination to go from strength to strength, to reach for perfection in the study of Torah, in *yirat shamayim*, in ethical behavior, in good *middot*, in *Chasidus*. As one peak was attained, one loftier swam into view, and this it was that spurred them on continually. In those far-off days people felt the compulsion always to be covering ground, always to be climbing up onto a higher rung, for what had been achieved thus far was surely but the entrance-chamber to much greater things, and their heart's desire was only to go higher, ever higher.

A person should constantly aim to perfect him/herself—the real thing—not settling for second best or anything that falls short of this goal. Yes, each according to his capacity but, within those limitations, "reaching for the stars." "For man is a tree of the field," (*Shoftim*, 20:19)—just as a living tree never stops growing, so must a person never stop growing.

Nowadays, we do not have such dreams—the yearning to be much more than one is, to go beyond and to go higher. We live without the dream of greatness, without these noble goals, (this is the way things are the world over and, sad to say, our Jewish brethren are no exception, particularly, with regard to learning Torah and keeping *mitzvot*). Now such a state of affairs is bound to sap the morale of our students, inhibiting the development of their own powers. Just as lack of appetite is a symptom of illness and debilitates the body, so to a much greater degree does the absence of ambition lead to the breakdown and decay of a person's spiritual capacities.

We must find ways to fix in the heart of the student the aspiration and the drive to ascend in holiness, in the knowledge of Torah, in the area of human relations, to beget in him the desire and the will to reach a higher level of spirituality, and at the same time, a profound discontent with his present level. We are speaking of something that applies to all students of every age, boys and girls alike.

A step in the right direction, certainly, is the organizing of festive meals to mark the completion of a chapter in *Gemara*, and the like, to publicize and give prominence to achievements of the individual and the group, with the aim and the effect of inspiring the students to set their sights ever higher and to build on what they have already achieved.

FEAR OF HEAVEN

In the heartland of Lubavitch they were so possessed by the fear of Heaven, the atmosphere was so saturated with it, that all discussion was superfluous. When there was fear of Heaven, discussion naturally tended towards loftier matters. Nowadays, however, the subject of the fear of Heaven must be restored to its rightful place at the top of the agenda.

ARDOR AND FEELING

There was a time when chasidim were noted for their depth of feeling; indeed, these were among the elemental qualities of *Chasidus*. Today, however, things are performed by rote—without fire, without heart. For example: *simcha*—not just to dance with one's feet, but to experience joy in the depths of the heart. Giving *tzedaka*—not just the physical act of giving, but giving with a radiant countenance, from feelings of purest compassion. And so it should be with everything else that we undertake, whether between a man and his Maker or man and his fellow.

PURITY

Boldly and unabashedly, we must raise the subject of purity—purity of thought, purity of speech, and especially purity in all one's acts; purity in all its connotations!

RESPONSIBILITY

We must explain to the students the concept of interdependency, "All Jews are guarantors for each other" (*Shevuot*, 39a); consequently, each of the students has a responsibility for his or her classmates, and, indeed, for every Jew. The student must be convinced of the fact that he is the guarantor of every Jew, and that he has a sacred duty to do whatever he can for the good of others, not, however, for their good alone, but for his own, too. For why—it will be demanded of him—did he not live up to his obligation to help others to the very best of his ability?

This is an important part of the education of a child, which will surely prove its worth later on in life as well, developing in him or her a powerful sense of responsibility towards others, whom he or she will try to steer onto the path of righteousness.

Again, in the eyes of his students the teacher must be a living embodiment of this principle. Thus, when the teacher comes to realize this, and acts the part of a guarantor for his own students, the change will surely not be lost on them, and they will want this to be a guiding principle of their own lives.

THE WHOLE AND THE PARTICULAR

It must be explained to the student that he or she is a part of the whole, depending on it as it depends upon them. If he or she is weakened, so is the entire organism—and if he or she is strong, the organism is automatically strengthened. The converse is equally true—the condition of the whole affects the particular—take the case of the soldier who is dropped into a war zone: if he is secure in the knowledge that the vast military machine in which he is little more than a name and a serial number does not in fact lose sight of him, or of the dangers he faces, then his morale remains high and he puts his heart and soul into the execution of his tasks.

CLEAVE TO HIS WAYS

We must take every opportunity to make the students aware of just how important a concept is contained in the words, "Cleave to His ways," (Rashi *R'eh*, 13:5).

The *Amidah* prayer is a "resource" for this purpose, as these examples show:

You are a warrior—the child must emulate the Creator and strive to be a warrior, to prevail over its "*yetzer hara*," (evil impulse).

Who revives the dead—he must strive to revive the person who is spiritually dead—specifically, the wicked, who even in his lifetime is considered to be dead, (*Berachot*, 18b). But this has to be done with the purest of motives, and when this is the case, the fact will be borne in upon the other so strongly that he will be helped to change his ways.

Who supports those who cannot stand—to support those who are in a state of spiritual collapse.

Who heals the sick—to heal those suffering from a spiritual sickness.

Who releases the confined—to liberate those who are spiritually "boxed in," who are no longer in control of their own lives.

You are holy—to infuse all he, or she, does with holiness.

Who desires that we return to Him—to do "*teshuvah*."

Gracious One who pardons abundantly—to forgive others unreservedly.

Who blesses His people Israel with peace—the love of one's fellow Jew and the unity of all Jews.

PRACTICAL *MITZVOT*

We must direct the steps of the student toward the fulfillment of practical *mitzvot*, and try to infuse him with a love for them.

We must make a "big deal" out of the performance of *mitzvot*, so that the student will go about doing them with enthusiasm and determination.

This lies at the very heart of *chinuch* and the teacher must endeavor to be a dynamic example of it.

JEWISH CUSTOMS

We must make it crystal clear to the students why the customs of the Jewish people are so precious, and underline the need for care and exactitude in their observance. The customs of the Jewish people are Torah, (*Tosafot*, "*Nifsal*," *Menachot*, 20b), verily a part of the Torah itself, and there are times when a *minhag*, a custom, has more force than the *halacha*—"Custom annuls halacha," (*Yerushalmi, Yebamot*, 12:1)

The Lubavitcher Rebbe, Rabbi Menachem M. Schneerson, often stressed the supreme virtue of Jewish customs, originating as they do in the highest levels of holiness. The Rebbe would bring proof from an explanatory passage in *Likkutei Torah* (*Derushim Lechag haSuccot*, 80,3)—the sublime level represented by the circuits of dancing with the Torah on *Simchat Torah*, the "*hakafot*-circuits," even though they are "merely" a *minhag*.

By way of illustration, there was a time when they would bake different *challot* for each festival, (round, long, ladder-shaped, and so on), and there should be a discussion of the reasons for this *minhag*, (see *Sefer Ta'amei HaMinhagim*, p. 550). Of course, a custom should also be observed in a spirit of acceptance of the yoke, but knowledge of the why's and wherefores adds an extra dimension to its observance.

We must not yield one inch of ground on this issue, for there are those who think that as long as it is only a question of custom, there really is no need to be concerned about its correct observance. Such an attitude often leads to the complete abandonment of *minhagim*.

AN EVIL COMPANION

Every day we recite in the morning *berachot*, ". . . that You should preserve us today and every day . . . from an evil companion." This has special relevance to children, and in fact goes to the heart of their world.

There are two reasons why we should avoid an evil companion: First, to keep him from harming us, to escape his influence and avoid the likelihood of being drawn onto his path.

Second, in order not to cause this evil companion even greater harm. When one child gets others into trouble, he or she is judged to be a bad influence and this stigma can be worse than any actual mischief that was caused. When the other child becomes his accomplice, the evil companion commits a further transgression, that of leading another into sin, and our Sages consider this to be worse than murdering him, (*Bamidbar Rabba*, 21:5).

Should the accomplice in question protest: "What if I *don't* listen to him, he'll simply find somebody else, and what difference does it make whether it is me or another—he'll still be called a bad influence!?

We have a two-pronged response: First—what if he doesn't succeed in finding another! Second—even if he does—at least it was not *you*. And we find a parallel to this in the mitzvah of *"ma'akeh,"*(the building of a parapet on the roof of one's house), whose purpose is to save from falling one who has a fall "coming to him," (*Teitsei*, 22:8, and in Rashi). In such a case, even though it is inevitable, I have to make sure that *I* am not the reason for his fall.

THE ESSENCE OF A JEW

The Alter Rebbe asserts in *Tanya*, (*Igeret Hakodesh*, 27), that the life of a *tzaddik* is not a life of the flesh at all but a life of the spirit, namely—faith, the fear of Heaven and love. Now this is no different from the essence and innermost being of *every* Jew, as we find written, (*Isaiah*, 60:21): "Your people are all righteous."

It is essential to explain to the student, in terms that he or she can fully grasp and assimilate, what, in essence, a Jew is. As and when the students come to see deeply into this essence they will strive to raise themselves, and grow in all those things that affect their innermost reality: in faith, in fear of G-d, and in love.

STRIKE WHILE THE IRON IS HOT!

We must exhort the students never to put off doing a good deed; it should be done without delay! Of this we learn, "When the opportunity to do a mitzvah presents itself, don't let it go sour on you." (Rashi, *Bo*, 12:17). The reasons for this are obvious enough:

First, circumstances may change, and the chance to perform the mitzvah may pass.

Second, if one acts promptly, the act, on the principle that "One mitzvah draws another in its wake," (*Avot*, 4:42), cannot fail to beget its own line of succession!

Third, the Rambam states, (*Hilchot Teshuvah*, 3:4), that with one mitzvah we may tilt the world, which is evenly balanced on the scales of judgment, towards (Divine) acquittal, and save it. How, then, can we put off acting a moment longer, when upon it depends the salvation of the whole world!?

Fourth, it all comes down to *alacrity*, which is nothing less than a foundation and starting-point of the *Shulchan Aruch*. And what *is* alacrity? Enthusiasm and zest, a joy-inducing state of mind—and when we act out of joy, our efforts are more likely, indeed, are guaranteed, to meet with success.

Again, the teacher must strive to be an exemplar of these virtues in the eyes of his students.

Rashi brings an illustration of this, (*Vayakhel*, 35:27): inasmuch as the heads of the tribes delayed their donations to the (construction of the) Tabernacle, the Torah in this passage—by omitting the letter "*yud*,"—spells their names deficiently. And remember, it is the "generation of knowledge" that we are talking of, the leaders and elders of Israel, no less, whose intention in doing what they did was certainly praiseworthy, (namely, that the *tzibbur*—the Congregation of Israel—should make its donations and then they, the leaders, would make up any shortfall), and yet they were judged to merit such a punishment.

THE GREATNESS OF THE CREATOR

Some of the time set aside for open discussion should be devoted to the subject of the greatness of the Creator, as it is reflected in Creation. There are various texts that recommend themselves, among them the *Shaarei Teshuvah* of Rabbenu Yona, Third Part, and *The Duties of the Heart, Sha'ar Habechinah*.

MASHIACH NOW!

The Lubavitcher Rebbe has called for a heightened awareness of Mashiach and the ultimate redemption—"We Want Mashiach Now!" The children should be asked if they ever stop to think about the meaning of this call; and if they answer in the affirmative—what has been the result, how has their thinking made a difference in the real world?

If there is truly a desire for Mashiach—the desire must express itself in practical terms, and everyone must ask themselves the question: what am I doing to hasten his coming?

In like vein, the students must be asked to give thought to what the coming of Mashiach will mean for them. The Rambam explains (*Hilchot Melachim*, 12:4) that the whole purpose of the coming of Mashiach is to enable us to learn Torah, free of all encumbrances. Hence, the question arises—nowadays, when we do have leisure and the obstacles to our Torah-learning have all but disappeared—do we seize the hour and *actually* learn more Torah?

HE WILL COMPEL ALL ISRAEL

The Rebbe has repeatedly quoted the statement of the Rambam, (*Hilchot Melachim*, 11:4), that Mashiach will compel the Jewish people to walk in the ways of Torah and buttress its "structures," this verily being the motive of our own activism, the outreach that we engage in, (the Mitzvah Campaigns, and so on). However, together with this, we also call for the practice of "inreach," working on *oneself* in the spirit of the words of the prophet: "Hide not yourself from your own flesh," (*Yeshayahu*, 58:7); and, as the Rebbe is fond of saying, we have room in our heads for both concepts. We must apply the principle of "he will compel," for example, to repel a not so positive thought when it rears its head, and in general—to reinforce and "fine tune" our relationship to Torah and the fear of Heaven.

The Rebbe explains in his talks that when we succeed in revealing the particular spark of Mashiach that exists in every Jew, we will bring on the supreme revelation of Mashiach our Righteous One.

CHAPTER 24
SHABBAT AND ROSH CHODESH

THE LAWS OF SHABBAT

The students must have a thorough knowledge of the laws of *Shabbat*. Although one might have taken the existence of such knowledge for granted, since *Shabbat* comes round regularly, week after week, many in fact lose their way in the complex particularity of its observance, and desecrate it through ignorance, especially in the area of "*muktzeh*," as we find explained in the *siddur* of the Alter Rebbe in "*Hilcheta Ravta l'Shabbata*," (name of a short halachic section printed towards the end of the *Siddur Tehilat Hashem*).

HELPING WITH THE PREPARATIONS FOR SHABBAT

The students should be taught—until it becomes ingrained in them—how important it is to make themselves useful about the house. I have in mind such pre-*Shabbat* activities as food-preparation, house-cleaning, setting up the *Shabbat* candles, and so on. A glance at the story related in the Talmud, (*Shabbat*, 119a) will help them appreciate the importance of this. Also, the *Shulchan Aruch* alludes to the fact (*Kitzur Shulchan Aruch*, 72:5) that the *Amoraim*, (sages of the Talmud), were far from considering it beneath themselves to help in the preparations for *Shabbat*.

In addition to the innate value of preparing to honor *Shabbat*, helping in the home on the eve of *Shabbat* also brings with it great benefits.

First, in a number of ways it enhances observance of the commandment to honor one's mother.

Second, the very fact that the child is motivated to help, and is alive to this aspect of *Shabbat*, will be a source of *nachas* and gratification to its mother.

Third, a mother has her hands full until the very last moment, when she lights the candles; with this additional manpower—her child— she will most likely be able to get all her work done, *and* have the candles lit, with time to spare, (at least—she will be on time).

ON THE THRESHOLD OF *SHABBAT*— TAKING NO CHANCES

There will always be a class of persons unable to let go of the idea that they have "time to play with," even after candle-lighting, especially when what is occupying them has a dimension of holiness to it. Such an attitude betrays a woeful disregard for the hallowed time approaching—no, much worse than that: indifference in the face of potential disaster!

KIDDUSH

The students must master the *nusach*, (the text of the benediction), of the *Kiddush*, and should make *Kiddush* at home every *Shabbat* evening. Hand-in-hand with this must go study of the laws of *Kiddush*, which should be part of the basic education of the sons of the house. Furthermore, on occasions when the father is absent, the son can step forward and make *Kiddush* in his stead.

THE *SHABBAT* TABLE

On Fridays, every teacher should entertain the class with a chasidic tale, (adapted to their age and level), or a short insight into the weekly *parsha*, suitable for repetition by the children at the *Shabbat* table, during the evening or the midday meal.

This should be standard practice in all of our institutions, all the more so when the children come from non-observant homes, in which case, especially, it promises to have lasting benefits.

First and foremost, when the parents are treated to a chasidic tale, or a beautiful idea derived from the weekly *parsha*, they will surely have a gratifying spiritual experience. When their children, who are the apple of their eye, make such an inspiring contribution to the *Shabbat* table, the parents sense what a difference this is making to their lives, which in turn leads them to be more positively disposed towards the school and the work of the school.

Furthermore, when such positive experiences become part and parcel of family life, they cannot help but bring about a change in the outlook of the parents, so that, when the student has to make up his mind whether or not to continue in that particular institution, the parents will discover that they are not opposed to the idea of his doing so.

HOW ARE THE *SHABBAT* EVENINGS SPENT?

The teacher should have some sense of how the student spends the long *Shabbat* evenings.

The father, worn-out and drowsy after the meal, may well be taking a nap. By the time he wakes up, the children have gone to bed. Alternatively, he may be absorbed in conversation with his wife, given that the week generally provides few opportunities for this staple of family life. The net result, however, is that the child is left too much to his or her own devices.

If the father would in fact be responsive to such an idea, he should be urged to spend some of this time learning with his children. If not, some other solution must be found to this problem of excessive leisure.

ATTENDING THE SYNAGOGUE

We must campaign tirelessly and be prepared to adopt any measure that will help us inspire or cajole parents into bringing their children to *shul* on *Shabbat*. Of course, such a visit must be arranged in the proper spirit—respect and awe for the holiness of the synagogue, awareness of the *halachot* governing synagogue procedure—as, for example, the prohibition on talking during prayer and Torah readings, and so on.

"GOING OVER" THE *SIDRA*

The children should be taught the cantillation—the *trup*—of both Torah and *Haftorah*. Once they reach the age of ten or above, they are to busy themselves with the mitzvah of reading the weekly *parsha* in its entirety, aloud—the Scriptural verses twice and the *Targum*, the Aramaic translation, once. The proper time for this is toward the end of the week or on *Shabbat* itself. It should also be made clear to them that they have until the following Tuesday to complete this task. If the time already passed and they forgot, they have until *Shemini Atzeret* to make up the portions that they omitted.

This is something which any *chinuch* worthy of the name must provide, and which will benefit the parents every bit as much as the child. Furthermore, a child so occupied will eventually achieve mastery and fluency in the *Chumash*. Therefore, they must let us know whether or not they have gone through the *parsha*. The institutions that circulated a questionnaire on this—were astonished and dismayed by the results. Nobody in the administrations concerned was able to find any consolation in the findings.

FILLING THE HOURS OF *SHABBAT*

There are places where teachers do not live in the same neighborhood as their pupils, meaning that the time available on *Shabbat* cannot be utilized to the full. Students are called "sons," and parents do not go off and leave their children an entire day without some form of supervision; rather, when they leave the house, they hire a caregiver to look after them. With that as our example, we should look for people with the appropriate skills who are willing to donate their time on *Shabbat*. As for remuneration, our Sages have stated, (*Chagiga*, 7a): (G-d says) "Just as I gave the Torah to you gratis and without charge, so are you to transmit it gratis and without charge," (and for this reason Torah teachers require a specific halachic dispensation—allowing them to receive payment).

There is a twofold purpose to conducting this *Shabbat* activity with the children. First, to protect them from undesirable influences. Second, to make of them vessels of holiness and light, and especially to provide them with the paradigm of an authentic *Shabbat*, and—to do this so well that it makes an indelible impression upon their hearts and minds.

How do we fill the hours of *Shabbat*? With "reviewing the *Sidra*," with the right kind of reading matter, with *Shabbat* gatherings, and so on.

UNDERSTANDING THE *HAFTORAH*

There must be a "no compromise" approach toward the regular learning of the *Haftorah*. We should learn it with the students every week and insure that they know the commentary well. (Needless to say, adults are not exempt from this requirement).

MESIBOS SHABBOS

The neighborhood *shul* or *cheder* would customarily hold a *mesibos Shabbos* gathering for the children, though this custom does not seem to have survived. Nevertheless, we must resuscitate it.

THE THIRD *SHABBAT* MEAL

Wherever it is the custom *not* to sit down to the third *Shabbat* meal, we should remind the students that they must eat *something* in order to fulfil what is an halachic obligation, recorded as such in the *Shulchan Aruch*. Not everyone can acquit himself by hearing or speaking words of Torah.

HAVDALAH

We must try to ensure that *Havdalah* is made in the homes of all our students on *Motzo'ei Shabbat*. By the same token, we must teach the students the *nusach* of the *Havdalah*, so that no one can blame their non-observance upon their ignorance.

V'YITEN LECHA

We should ascertain whether or not the students say *"V'yiten Lecha"* on *Motzo'ei Shabbat*. In many circles its recital is neglected. Granted that it is "only" a *minhag*—custom—but it is printed in the *siddur*, and there are many sound reasons for its recital.

I recall that once while still in Riga, on *Motzo'ei Shabbat*, I came into the presence of the Rebbe, Rabbi Yosef Yitzchak, and saw his son-in-law, the Rebbe, Rabbi Menachem Mendel, reciting *V'yiten Lecha* from a *siddur*, in the quiet, self-effacing manner that was the Rebbe's hallmark. The scene made an unforgettable impression on me.

MOTZO'EI SHABBAT

The teacher should try to find out how the students occupy themselves after *Shabbat* is ended, where and with whom he or she spends their leisure time. The teacher should do what he can to influence them to spend the time, especially of the long winter nights, in a constructive and fruitful manner.

We could perhaps make use of a questionnaire to throw some light on the *Shabbat* situation. The children can indicate how they spend their time on *Shabbat*. This information they should bring to their teacher on Sunday, with their parents' signature attached.

SAFEGUARDING OUR INVESTMENT

Who can be indifferent to the fate of his handiwork? And who would not turn pale at the thought that all that he has worked and striven for could be ruined in a day? Take, then, a student with whom his teacher has shared his knowledge, investing in the process all his energy and skill. And consider how, at the end of the school day, when he is no longer under supervision, the baneful atmosphere of the street can wreak havoc with all that has been so laboriously achieved in the classroom. Even a single moment spent beyond its pale can do a great deal of harm—as in the case of one who goes from a warm room into the cold air and risks catching a chill, or even a fever; as in the case of a soldier, crouching in his fox-hole with the bullets whistling overhead—who need only show his face to have his life snuffed out.

To what conclusion does this bring us? Obviously, the student must be kept busy every hour of the day, every day of the week, and particularly on *Shabbat*!

SHABBAT M'VARECHIM

Before the onset of *Shabbat M'varechim*, the *Shabbat* before the New Month, it is wise to alert the students to it, explain to them the significance of the blessing for the new month and inform them of its exact date and of additions or changes to the prayer service.

In addition, older students should have the *molad*, the "birth" of the moon, the method for calculating its appearance, and so on, explained to them.

These details may usefully be shared with the students' families, given that a mother may not always be aware of the new month that's approaching and will wait for her husband's return from *shul* on *Shabbat M'varechim* in order to be told when it will take place.

I once asked a child if he had made the blessing of the New Month and he replied that he had, but he thought that *that Shabbat* was itself *Shabbat Rosh Chodesh*, not *Shabbat M'varechim haChodesh*. Similarly, it emerged that he did not properly understand the whole subject of the blessing of the New Month, nor was he aware on what day the new month fell.

ROSH CHODESH

We must put the celebration of *Rosh Chodesh* on a loftier plane, and enhance awareness of it as a special and exalted day, similar to a *chag*—a festival—even though work is permitted on it. This can be accomplished by providing a special lunch, at which tasty dishes are to be served, impressing upon the children the fact that this feast is in honor of *Rosh Chodesh*.

KIDDUSH LEVANAH

Let us encourage the students to recite the blessing of the New Moon regularly. This can be rewarded with prizes, etc. When the students happen to be at school, it is best if they say the blessing of the moon all together in the same place.

CHAPTER 25
ELUL

SHOFAR AND TEHILLIM

Beginning with *Rosh Chodesh Elul*, the students must have the opportunity to hear the blowing of the *shofar* daily.

Boys of nine and above—his ninth year heralding a new epoch in a boy's life—must recite on every day of *Elul* three chapters of *Tehillim*, as is our custom. Students below this age—should recite particular verses in *Tehillim*, as a reminder that they are now in the month of *Elul*.

THE MONTH OF RECKONING

It should be explained to the students that *Elul* is the month of reckoning, the month of soul-searching. Try to make everyone, students and teachers alike, feel the atmosphere of *Elul*, finding ways to intensify it so that their preparations gather momentum as *Rosh Hashana* draws near. This is also the purpose of the blowing of the *shofar* during the month of *Elul*—to give this month, which will culminate in the Days of Awe, an even stronger hold upon our consciousness.

ATMOSPHERE OF *ELUL*

There was a time when the atmosphere of *Elul* was almost palpable; the solemn atmosphere of a people making ready to repent, an atmosphere of preparation and expectancy. The sound of the *shofar* on *Elul* is the reveille of the conscience. So it was even among the simple and the unlettered of our brothers and sisters. Everyone knew that *Rosh Hashana* was drawing near, that now was the time to repent. Before the day itself we felt in the very atmosphere that Judgment Day was upon us, that our repentance could no longer be delayed. Each one strove with his conscience, vanquishing or vanquished, according to the level of the contest, the intensity of the struggle.

Even those who continually put off this time of reckoning— when *Rosh Hashana* approached—could not avoid the sensation of something drawing inexorably closer. . . .

But how do things stand now, we ask?!

We have a tough task ahead of us: to attempt to retrieve that world of feeling, to return to that splendor and that awesomeness, in the hope that present realities may, in some measure, bear comparison with our glorious past....

All of which calls to mind the well-known talk of the Rebbe, Rabbi Yosef Yitzchak of Lubavitch, *(Likkutei Dibburim*, Vol. 1, p. 230), in which he describes the *Elul* atmosphere that was unique to Lubavitch. Indeed, the Rebbe, Rabbi Menachem Mendel Schneerson, has always argued that if such descriptions have come down to us at all, it is solely for the purpose of inspiring us to recreate in the here-and-now, to experience for ourselves, the world of feeling they so vividly describe!

HILCHOT *TESHUVAH*

During the entire month of *Elul*, the detailed study of the laws of *teshuvah* (those codified by Rambam, for example) should be the order of the day, and the topic of *teshuvah* the burden of our conversation. No less than with the laws of *tzitzit* and *tefillin*, do we possess a body of laws pertaining exclusively to *teshuvah*, and all of us, young and old, are required to immerse ourselves in them.

Similarly, there should be wide-ranging study and discussion of ethical material.

HOW TO DO *TESHUVAH*

When we turn the performance of a mitzvah into something mechanical and uninspired, the fact that it falls short is glaringly obvious, and yet the mitzvah has been performed. Not so with the mitzvah of *teshuvah*—for if we do this mitzvah in such a manner, it is as if we have performed no mitzvah at all! The individual concerned does not know *what teshuvah* is, nor how to accomplish it. Since he has not studied the *halachot* of *teshuvah*, his efforts to fulfil the basic mitzvah will be frustrated. To whom should he be compared? To one who wishes to fulfill the mitzvah of *etrog* and, not having a clue how to proceed, takes in his hand a lemon rather than an *etrog*!

FEELINGS OF *TESHUVAH*

Rosh Hashana and *Yom Kippur* are bound up with *teshuvah*. The problem is, that we approach *teshuvah* in the manner of a sleepwalker, as if it were actually something that could be accomplished in our sleep. As to what *teshuvah* is—the definition is not the least bit abstract. We must take the mitzvah of *teshuvah*, give it substance and form, and fill with it the mind and heart of the child. Then, surely, will his tears well up upon the recital of *selichot*, upon the sounding of the *shofar*, and when the Day of Judgment itself arrives . . . each child according to his or her age and capacity. All of us must sincerely want and strive to be better than we are, better than we have been.

TESHUVAH AND CONTRITION

Contrition is a vital component of *teshuvah*—indeed, it is a formal requirement. *Chasidus* explains that sadness must be rooted out, whereas the bitterness arising from contrition is an indispensable element in the service of G-d and has its time and its place.

TESHUVAH OUT OF JOY

One of the innovations of *Chasidus* is the teaching that *teshuvah* is possible even when one is in a state of joy—in the spirit of the Psalm (2:12), ". . . and rejoice when there is trembling," (that the two states, joy and trepidation, may indeed co-exist). When the greatness of *teshuvah* is grasped, its efficacy for every man and woman whatever their circumstances, and they actually do *teshuvah*—then this very fact must bring them to a level of ecstatic joy.

CHAPTER 26
TISHREI

THE MONTH OF *TISHREI*

When the month of *Tishrei* goes the way it should, the whole year goes the way it should.

THE DAYS OF AWE

There was a time when you could feel in the very air a hushed expectancy, as the Days of Awe, and all that they portended, drew ever nearer. As day yielded to darkness and to the holiness of the new day, an atmosphere of great solemnity would descend upon the synagogue. On the following day, when the one appointed to blow the *shofar* began to recite "*Lamenatzeach*," before the blowing of the first blast, everyone present, even those ignorant of the meaning of the words, would start to cry, for the Day of Judgment was at hand.

It was no different during the Ten Days of Repentance. Then there was *Erev Yom Kippur* and *Yom Kippur*—at the beginning of *Kol Nidrei*, in every corner of the *shul* the atmosphere of holiness and purity was something you could touch with your hand—who, then, could be unaware that today was *Yom Kippur*? And at *Ne'ilah*, every soul knew that it was now the eleventh hour, that in a little while the gates would be locked and that *teshuvah* could not be put off a moment longer. Afterwards—came the true and profound joy of the singing of the "march" that followed *Ne'ilah*. Truly, these were days unlike any others, marked by the service of G-d, earnestness and sincerity, the abandonment of all pretense—an altogether different atmosphere.

And now . . .? We do no more than go through the motions; at the *climax of the year*.

Then what is to be done?—As I see it, rather than throw up our arms in despair at such a pitiful decline, we must stage a revolt: *things must be restored to their former splendor!*

SUCCAH

We must see to it that no child's home will be without a *succah*.

CHOL HAMOED

Students should attend school for two hours every day on *Chol Hamoed*, for prayer and for study. A system of teacher rotation will make this feasible.

When *Chol Hamoed* is longer—falling in the middle of the week—a variety of programs should be put together, to make the most of the extra time. The framework for this should be one of communal learning under supervision.

We must see to it that the time is not wasted. A source of endless worry is the contact the children may have with the culture of the street and the unclean atmosphere of the street—the depravity bred of its sights and sounds. Who knows what harm might not befall them if we fail to be vigilant!

We must encourage the students to join a *minyan* for all three daily prayers of *Chol Hamoed*.

TEACHER-PARENT CONFERENCES

During *Chol HaMoed* we should hold an informal teacher-parent conference, all in the spirit of the festival, cordial and welcoming—to consider different ideas and suggestions for improving the level of scholarship, general conduct, *middot*, and so on.

CHAPTER 27
PASSOVER AND *SEFIRAT HAOMER*

THE LAWS OF PASSOVER

Before *Pesach* the laws of the Festival must be reviewed with the children. The sounder the grasp they have of these laws the greater the influence they are likely to have upon their parents. Additionally, the children should be in a position to give over different explanations and commentaries from the *Hagaddah* during the course of the *seder*.

MORID HA-TAL AND *TEIN BERACHAH*

The details of the laws governing the recital of the above must be taught in class.

PIRKEI AVOT

At the conclusion of Passover we begin the study of *Pirkei Avot*.

(The Rebbe re-introduced the custom of continuing with the recitation of these chapters every *Shabbat* afternoon throughout the summer months, and would himself stay in *shul* to do so).

We expect every child to have a thorough knowledge of *Pirkei Avot*. It is an ethical work and as such is concerned with righteous behavior and *middot*; therefore we must not allow the study of it to degenerate into an empty parroting of phrases.

Rather, everything must be brought down to a practical level, to the level of daily behavior. *Pirkei Avot* should be on the curriculum of every class and in each lesson one specific point should be chosen for intensive discussion.

SEFIRAT HAOMER

Since we begin the Counting of the *Omer* at a time when the students are not at school, the best course for teachers to adopt is to review this mitzvah before the Passover vacation. They should survey the mitzvah itself and also point out how it is a preparation for *Matan Torah*—the Giving of the Torah—and for the Festival of *Shavuot*.

"COUNTING" IN CLASS

The Counting of the *Omer* should take place every morning in class, without a *beracha*, to give the student who forgot to count at night the chance to do so now. In this way he will be able to continue counting thereafter with a *beracha*, (in accordance with *halacha*).

RECTIFICATION OF MIDDOT

In the text of *Sefirat HaOmer* we say, "(May it be Your will, L-rd our G-d) that in the merit of the *Sefirat HaOmer* which I performed today, the blemish that I have caused in the *Sefirah* be rectified," namely, that a specific rectification be carried out by virtue of the *Sefirah*. This matter can be explained very simply, in terms of the perfecting of the *middot*.

In the chasidic discourse—*Usefartem Lachem*, printed in *Sefer Maamarim*, (*Chasidic Discourses*, Vol. 1, Kehot, 1986), by Rabbi Yosef Yitzchak Schneersohn of Lubavitch, there is an explanation of the subject of the *sefirot* that is accessible to all. Similarly, in *Tanya*, (*Igeret Hakodesh*, 15,) the ten *sefirot* are explained in a simple way, using the examples of a father studying with his son and a teacher with his student.

The days of the Counting of the *Omer* should be oriented, in a variety of ways, toward the correcting and the improvement of the *middot*.

PREPARATION FOR THE GIVING OF THE TORAH

During this period, it is advisable to speak with the students every day on the subject of the Counting of the *Omer* and *Matan* Torah, and to impress upon them the urgency of preparing themselves for *Matan* Torah.

One such method of preparation is—diligence in Torah, letting not a single moment go to waste, (and we see, at the beginning of *Tanya*, how powerfully the prohibition against neglecting the study of Torah is stressed).

STUDY OF THE FORTY-EIGHT ATTRIBUTES

During the days of *Sefirah*, it is appropriate to study the forty-eight attributes by which the Torah is acquired. This can perhaps be inserted into the daily curriculum, so that every day one specific attribute is studied—thus, over the course of *sefirah*, all forty-eight will be traversed.

The Torah must be acquired actively. Every act of acquisition has its legal instrument, while the Torah has, for itself, the forty-eight attributes by which it is acquired, as enumerated in the *Mishnah* (*Avot*, 6:6). These points should be raised during *Sefirah*, so that in reality there will be an acquisition of the Torah—a taking of possession in the fullest sense—come the time of *Matan* Torah.

The students should have these forty-eight attributes "at their fingertips" and know and live them in the depths of their being.

THE THREE PILLARS

On the days when *Pirkei Avot* is studied, the teacher should speak of the three pillars on which the world rests—Torah, Divine service, (which is prayer), and loving-kindness, (ch.1, *mishnah* 2). The sections making up this course can be based on a series of talks—the first devoted to Torah, explaining the primacy of Torah; the second, to actual service; the third, to loving-kindness. Each "pillar" should be dealt with at length, illustrated and elucidated within the framework of the world in which we live, providing every day different perspectives on the same theme. We must establish in those we teach the firm conviction that the foundation of their "little world"—their microcosm—is the three pillars. Therefore, this concept must be internalized, made an integral part of their own personalities, in the following manner:

Torah—What is learned must be brought down to the plane of daily, practical existence, and knowing that "his world" rests upon this pillar—Torah, his or her Torah study is elevated to a much higher level.

Avodah—prayer—cannot be effectual if it does not possess the element of "Know before Whom you stand." One who prays must know he is praying to G-d—the King of the universe—Who has the power to grant his requests; and when he does—when he knows to Whom he prays and for what he prays—his prayer is transfigured.

Loving-kindness—even if the recipient is not a *"mensch"* and withholds his thanks, this will not inhibit the flow of *"chesed,"* since the giver is aware that his act is not something external to himself but bears upon his own vital interests, that it puts his own world on a more secure footing.

By the same token, the principles embodied in these three pillars must be practiced every single day.

In the case of *Torah*, something must be learned every day, and how much more effective this will be if it can be done immediately after prayer. With *prayer*, the goal is to pray with a *minyan* at all times.

Loving-kindness expresses itself, at the simplest level, in the giving of *tzedaka*, at the very least a nickel or a dime every day.

CHAPTER 28
SENIOR YESHIVOT

ESSENTIAL *HALACHOT*

One of our fundamental tasks is to set up a learning schedule devoted to the essential *halachot* of *Orach Chaim*, with a view to giving the students a solid foundation in these core subjects. In fact, the Rebbe himself frequently encouraged this.

Most appropriate to this type of learning is the system of paired study, each pair concentrating on a different *halacha*. Particular emphasis should be placed on *Hilchot Tefillah*—whose observance is commonly found to be sub-standard, simply because of ignorance of the details of these *halachot*.

PRAYER

The service of prayer plays a central role in *Chasidus*, as well as being pivotal in the *sichot* of the Rebbe. Yet prayer—proceeding in a spirit of inwardness and quiet reflection—has become a "lost art." We must turn things around. To begin with, emphasis should be placed on learning the laws of prayer, something in which everyone should be proficient.

Students must be broken of the habit of wandering to all four corners of the room during prayer. They must be taught to pray in one place with the proper self-control, and to put into practice what they have learned by praying with a *minyan*. In an institutional setting it is possible to have everyone begin praying together, with the requisite standard of concentration, enunciating the words, and in putting their hearts into what they are doing. Similarly, they must be prompt in responding *Amen* and *Amen yehei shemei rabbah*, (and the study of the laws of prayer will help here too). This study should be supplemented with the study of *ma'amarim* which deal with the subject of prayer.

When the senior *yeshivot* bring their level of prayer up to standard, the middle and junior *yeshivot* will follow suit, imitating their self-control in prayer, and their enunciation of the words in a strong and clear voice, and so on and so forth.

A FIXED PLACE

All the students of the yeshivah, across the entire age range, must be made aware of the stipulation in the *Shulchan Aruch*, (*Kitzur Shulchan Aruch*, 12:10), that one have a regular place for prayer, even when praying at home. Once the reasons for this are understood, there will be a meaningful difference in the way the students pray.

We must institutionalize this practice, so that every student has his *makom*—his "place"—and we no longer have to tolerate the spectacle of students wandering from place to place in the study-hall.

REVIEWING THE *PARSHAH*

All students must be made aware that reading through the entire *parshah*, (as explained in Chapter 24), is an obligation of the Torah. At the same time, we must identify all those who do not yet know the *trup*—the cantillation—of the Torah reading, and especially of the *Haftorah*, and make sure that they are given the help they need to acquire this skill.

"SEE NO EVIL"

On occasion we need to impress upon the students the importance of protecting themselves against thoughts and sights that may lead to mischief and harm. Many are the situations and circumstances that call for the utmost vigilance on their part.

THE PROHIBITION AGAINST *YICHUD*

The senior students must be made aware—with all necessary delicacy and tact—of the important place occupied by the *halachot* of *yichud*. There is widespread ignorance of this subject. Some go so far as to consider *yichud* little more than a *minhag*, consequently they downplay its importance, and there are those who do not even suspect the existence of such a prohibition.

Sometimes, when a young man begins dating, he meets with the girl in her parents' house, and the parents go out and leave them on their own, with the inevitable result that they transgress the *issur* of *yichud*; (sometimes the boy will be too embarrassed to leave, or think it impolite, etc.). The fact is, a couple may find themselves in breach of the *issur* for any number of reasons.

Serious as the subject of *yichud* is, *per se*, it is also implicated in a variety of problems.

Accordingly, much thought should go into working out an approach to this subject that will ensure that the essentials are put across without our exceeding the bounds of modesty and good taste.

TOILING IN TORAH

We must demonstrate the elemental virtue that lies in toiling in Torah, as explained in *Hemshech* of 5666 [1906] on *Parshat Toldot*. The Rebbe frequently takes this point up in his *sichot*, pointing to the example of the Arizal, who when studying *halachah* took on a lion-like ferocity, the perspiration pouring from him as he strained with all his might. (See *Likkutei Sichot*, vol. 9, p. 252).

GOOD *MIDDOT*—CHARACTERISTICS

At regular intervals we should seek to highlight one particular good characteristic, going into it deeply—together with sources and source-references—in effect, providing the students with a *shiur* on this topic. In general, there is a vast amount to be said on the subject of good *middot*, as well as on inter-personal issues, an area of knowledge which fails to receive the attention that it merits.

What is *Chasidus* when the heart of it is missing—fear of Heaven, good *middot*, and living with *Chasidus*, and the ways of *Chasidus*!?

WORKING ON ONESELF

Chasidus demands that we be honest with ourselves. Thus, it behooves a man to look into his heart and acknowledge the reality of his feelings. Only then can he put the necessary changes into effect. *Chasidus* returns to this theme over and over again, and the student must be no stranger to it: that one must *ton mit zich*—work hard at making himself a better person.

COMMUNITY SERVICE AND SELF-IMPROVEMENT

Community service with our fellow Jews is a categorical imperative. Indeed, students who go on *mivtza'im* every Friday, visiting offices, shops and other locations, accomplish a great deal. Often the work of these youngsters has profound reverberations—what we see of it and are able to quantify is only the "tip of the iceberg."

This *must* be supplemented, however, by work on oneself at all levels: thought, speech and action, as well as by the striving for good *middot*. And there must be no self-deception. Everyone can find something in himself that cries out for improvement, much though this may vary from individual to individual.

Regarding the ritual sacrifices, it is stated: "...with all your offerings you shall offer salt," (*Vayikra*, 2:13). Salt is symbolic of longevity, durability, "... a covenant of salt forever," (*Korach*, 18:19). But, in spite of its usefulness, there is no *korban* of salt alone. Similarly, working with others is indeed imperative, such work comes under the category of "salt," which in itself cannot be a sacrifice. You have to "sacrifice" yourself, then there is additionally the salt that gives relish and strength to everything.

YIRAT SHAMAYIM

In Lubavitch of yesteryear the very atmosphere was permeated with the fear of G-d. Indeed, this feeling was omnipresent, so much so that discussion tended to take place on an altogether higher plane. In today's world, however, no such phenomenon is to be found, and if *yirat shamayim* is to be a real concept for the students, and play a serious role in their lives, there is going to have to be a great deal of heart-to-heart discussion and a return to basics.

ARDOR AND FEELING

Chassidim were once known for putting their heart into everything they did, as well as for their friendly demeanor. Nowadays, however, everything is done in a mechanical fashion, with little heart or real feeling.

Joy, for example, should register in the heart—an actual sensation of joy, of which the physical act of dancing is only the outward expression and not the essence.

Charity—to take another example—consists not just in the physical act of giving, but in giving happily, and in a sympathetic manner.

This is the standard to aim for with every mitzvah, whether between man and G-d or between man and man.

LIFE AND WARMTH

There was a time when the yeshivas were places abounding with vitality and warmth, not to mention tremendous excitement over every aspect of Judaism, Torah and *mitzvot*. Today, we, the educators, no less than the students, have our work cut out for us not only to bring warmth into our own yeshivas but to go the extra mile and have our inspiration penetrate to other yeshivas as well.

RESTORING THINGS TO THEIR FORMER GLORY

We must put heart and soul into the attempt to restore the glory that was, as in the heyday of Lubavitch and our yeshivas, from the time of our origins to the present. This sentiment was expressed once by the Rebbe in a note, (7th Elul, 5740/1980):

"Lubavitch has been in existence for some 200 years," that is, nothing has changed! and this is his will: that we should strive to return things to their former glory. The Rebbe wants every one of our students to be aware of the fact that he is a student belonging to Lubavitch, even when he walks in the street, clearly showing this in the way that he thinks, speaks and acts, and in the good attributes that he exemplifies.

From time to time the students of Tomchei Temimim must have the opportunity to lay eyes upon the image of inwardness, the vision of spirituality, that is a true Chassid, a true "*tamim*," (one who is altogether single-minded and complete in his devotion to Torah and *mitzvot*), for this is our inner reality, the authentic countenance of Lubavitch. We must dwell on the need for more inwardness, more inner content, in everything that we do; the need to inject more Chasidic vitality and urgency into every piece of business that we transact, every project—praying, doing good to another Jew—whatever it may be—with passionate involvement.

And yet—all this must be done without self-delusion, without fancying oneself to be what one is not, without giving oneself airs.

PILPUL OF THE STUDENTS

It used to be a regular feature of yeshivah life that, once a week, in the presence of his peers, a student would deliver a *pilpul*—the intricate analysis of a Talmudic theme. We should restore this practice wherever it has been allowed to lapse.

LEARNING *CHASIDUS*

Chasidus should be studied in a manner that enables the student to impart to others what he has learned; simply to review the material, as if it were an academic exercise, is to miss the point entirely!

THE MEANING OF THE WORDS

During the course of the students' study of *Chasidus*, they will no doubt be asked to examine the meaning and order of the daily prayers. This being so, to know the meaning of the prayers is of the very essence. *Do* they know the meaning of *Ezehu M'komon?* And what of the other sections of the *davening?* A verse from Prophets or Writings that appears in the order of prayer should at least be understood in the plain sense, as it is explained by Rashi and the *Metzudat David*.

CHAPTER 156 OF *SHULCHAN ARUCH*

The students must be urged to study Chapter 156, in the *Shulchan Aruch* of the Alter Rebbe, the section in which are to be found the *halachot* pertaining to many ways in which we interact with our fellow man during the course of the day. The Alter Rebbe had a clear purpose in mind when he placed this chapter in the section of *Orach Chaim*, (laws of conduct in daily life), immediately after the laws of prayer, in this way making it coincide with the beginning of a person's daily routines.

HAYOM YOM

The study of *Hayom Yom* should be stressed, with the accent put on translating its lessons into action.

FREE LOAN SOCIETY

The Rebbe suggested that there should be a free loan society for the students. In general they need to be better informed as to the nature and function of a *g'mach*. In due course, one of them should be appointed *gabbai*, to administer the fund in accordance with the Rebbes instructions.

STUDY OF THE RAMBAM

When we study the Rambam's halachic writings and find an ethical teaching, (for example, at the end of the *halacha*), time must be set aside for more intensive study of this teaching. This is in fact the practice of the Rebbe, who during his talks on Rambam always gives close attention to points bearing on the perfection of the *middot*.

No matter where one turns to in the Rambam's halachic writings, one finds practical applications to real-life situations. For example, the prohibition against *geneivat daat*—lit. stealing the mind: the deception of another through concealing or misrepresenting one's intentions towards him, or something that concerns him. Instances of this are only too common in everyday life, and because we treat this prohibition with such recklessness, we find ourselves in breach sometimes of a rabbinic, sometimes of an actual Torah prohibition connected with it.

As with the Rambam, so with the Tractate of the Talmud studied in the yeshivah—at many points it will touch directly upon issues in our daily lives. We must be sure to explore the lessons it teaches in all their ramifications.

We must not fall into the error of those who do not learn *aggadata*, (the non-halachic portions of the Torah), or who only give them a passing glance, considering them unworthy of serious attention.

FROM EVERYTHING THAT'S LEARNED—A LESSON

In every statement and in every topic that is studied it is possible to find a guide to action. Accordingly, we must look thoroughly into the question—what is the most instructive approach to take? The portion of *Tanya* that is learned daily as part of *Chitas*—*Chumash, Tehillim* and *Tanya*—should be looked at in the same light: after it has been studied, the bearing that it has upon practical *avodah* should be made to stand out as boldly as possible. This is the method most likely to lead to action. The same applies to the study of Talmud, Rambam, etc.

The students must be given the tools to practice what they are taught, as the saying has it: *"Vos hut Torah dich gelerent?"*— What has the Torah taught *you*?

LEARNING A *MA'AMAR* BY HEART

The memorization and reviewing of *Chasidus* is of vital importance, as explained in *Chasidus*, (*Likkutei Torah*, the beginning: *Vahadarta*). However, one must be certain to go into the subject as deeply as possible, as opposed to simply remembering or recording it—like a photographic image, which can be stored in the memory without necessarily touching or affecting the person in a serious manner.

Everyone learning to review *Tanya* and *Chasidus* by heart, should be taught to focus on the *maamar* and discover in the topic that he is reviewing the way in which it uniquely "speaks to him." This directive applies to students at all levels of the yeshiva, even to a *bar mitzvah* boy who, although he is struggling manfully with the *ma'amar*, finds it a little strange or even inaccessible. The challenge, all the same, is to bring him to feel that it is relevant to him, so that he comes away from the study of it richer for the experience, having learned the meaning of it for his own life and having made it his own in the process.

If we teach this approach to the students, the teachers themselves will be given a tremendous lift when they see how well their instruction has borne fruit.

CHATTING, NOT HARANGUING

We should of course have regular talks with the students—*shmuessen* I prefer to call them—friendly chats with a specific class, or a looser grouping of students. At such a time, the teacher should take one particular point from a *ma'amar* currently being studied and show how it is possible to translate it into practice on a daily basis.

THE PERSONAL TOUCH

Each and every student deserves to be regarded and catered to as an individual. Remember, the goal is to win him over, not to alienate him. There must be a caring attitude towards each student, just as if he or she were one's own son or daughter. (See Chapter 4).

The time and place must be found to take the student aside and spur him on to greater things, spiritually, as well as helping him focus on some specific character defect. At the same time, the approach should be discreet, guarding the student's privacy. These matters can be raised during study, or at the end of the week, at the time when the teacher happens to be talking with the student, or on *erev Rosh Chodesh*, (*Yom Kippur Katan*, a time of atonement), the month of *Elul*, *erev Rosh HaShana*, and so on. This talk should serve as an "injection," to immunize against "infection," and should be followed with a "booster shot"—a story or tale.

SENSITIVITY TO AVODAH

Room must be made in the curriculum for the study of *avodah ma'amarim*—material that touches upon *yirat shamayim*, the beautification of *mitzvot*—for example, Chapter 41 of *Tanya*, *Igeret HaTeshuva*, *Derech Chaim*, and so on.

Seforim whose subject is religious awe, such as *Reishit Chochma*, and *Sha'arei Teshuva* of Rabbenu Yona, should be studied, together with whatever deals in the most direct way with the fear of Heaven, (not that this should be integrated into the regular *seder*, for which we have no precedent in the yeshivah's history, although I *have* heard from *mashpi'im* that such *seforim* were in fact studied privately).

When the students learn *Chasidus*, the possibility exists that they will learn the wisdom, but not the system of conduct that can be derived from it—its ultimate goal and good. The students are left only with what might be termed "book learning," while the critical component, the *yirat shamayim*, is missing. They have not really been touched, therefore, and it is for the *mashpiah* to acquaint them with the method that allows concepts and ideas to be translated into concrete deeds. By contrast, when *yirat shamayim* and service in a practical sense are approached in a direct manner—a much stronger impression is left upon the mind, and we have reason to believe that the study will then lead to action and to feelings of *yirat shamayim*.

Everything having to do with Torah brings with it a quantum of *yirat shamayim*, but to what extent depends upon the form and character of the study. If during study the holiness of the Torah is felt and apprehended, then this can indeed lead to fear and awe; but if we study the topic and the wisdom in it only as an intellectual exercise—even though it remains the Torah of Hashem, *yirat shamayim* will nevertheless not be among its active ingredients. Even when the "revealed" Torah—explicit laws and principles—is being studied, it is not enough simply to learn the wisdom in the thing, for the inner dimension, *yirat shamayim*, must also be present. And in what does this consist? In nothing less than the power that this knowledge possesses to transform the individual who acquires it.

VARIOUS SPECIALTIES IN TORAH

There are various more specialized pursuits within the Torah that virtually remain a closed book and in which it is hard to find knowledgeable individuals—for example, Hebrew grammar, *Midrash*, *Ein Yaakov*, the history of the Jewish people, and so on. It is no secret that the Rebbe, Rabbi Yosef Yitzchak, fully expected the students to study and be proficient in *Nach*, Hebrew grammar and penmanship, as well as Jewish history.

We must therefore expand our curriculum to include these subjects—albeit outside of the regular yeshiva schedule, or at times when there is no formal yeshiva program. Most effective for this purpose will be the teaming of students into pairs, each pair pursuing the speciality of its choice and studying it in sufficient depth to arrive at a reasonable degree of mastery.

For example, one pair might focus its energies on various aspects of "*drush*"—homiletic interpretation—to be found in *ma'amarim* and *sichot*. The study of these subjects is crucial, since, sooner or later, the student will be expected to give a *shiur* for the layman, in *Ein Yaakov* or in homiletics, (one recalls the statement in *Tanya*—*Igeret HaKodesh*, chap. 23—that most of the

182 The Educator's Handbook

secrets of the Torah are hidden in the pages of *Ein Yaakov* and that its study atones for one's sins).

Another pair might lean more towards philosophy and faith, which is the subject of such works as *Duties of the Heart*.

Another idea worth considering is to put together an anthology—passages culled from various *seforim* and dealing with various topics—to contain easy material as well as some which is more challenging—and to develop out of this a study manual, for the use of the group or the individual.

Where did the idea not to study such things come from? Did some committee form itself for just such a purpose, deliberate, and in its wisdom banish them from the curriculum?!

In our institutions we must have students who are distinguished in a variety of fields—in *Ein Yaakov*, in *Midrash*, Jewish history, and so forth.

THE STUDY OF *NACH*

We expect the students to know the names of the Prophets, their general dates, the dates of any specific *Navi*, and so forth. They must be got into the habit of learning *Nach* by themselves. According to *Hayom Yom*, (19th *Adar Rishon*), Chassidim would review *Nach* every day while in the act of winding their *tefillin* and putting away their *talleisim*. Students should learn at the very least those chapters of *Tehillim* that are included in the daily prayers. A student who studies *Mishle*, (Proverbs), for example, will know how cautious he must be when mingling with the crowd, and will be quick to spot the pitfalls and stumblingblocks that litter the path of the unwary.

THE STRENGTHENING OF FAITH

I asked a Rosh Yeshiva how matters stood with regard to *emunah* and he had to confess that the picture was not a glossy one.

It seems to me that the missing element is the "Know what to answer," (*Avot*, 2:12). When a student is challenged on matters of faith, he tries to give a good account of himself, but is prey to all kinds of doubts, lacks fervor and dynamism; a want of force and spirit to subdue "the heretic within." For the plain truth is that, no less than heresy and apostasy, *avodah zarah*, the spirit of idolatry, is always with us in one guise or another.

What better response can there be than to immerse oneself in literature that strengthens faith, including the *ma'amarim*: *Ha'amanut Elokut* and *Achdut Hashem* in the Tzemach Tzedek's *Derech Mitzvotecha*. (In Riga there was a *baal teshuvah* who was in search of material to strengthen his faith, and the Rebbe, Rabbi Yosef Yitzchak, told him to study *Ha'amanat Elokut*).

ASPIRING TO THE RABBINATE AND TO *CHINUCH*

We must fire the student with the ambition, and the determination, to serve the Jewish people as a rabbi—a true *rav*, one who exercises genuine authority in his city and brings about fundamental improvements in the institutional life of city and *kehilla*. Much can be accomplished in the sphere of the Rabbinate, and even a casual glance at the state of Judaism today will bring home the importance of this point. Regrettably, however, we do not see any evidence among the students of a burning desire to serve in the Rabbinate.

Similarly—and it cannot be sufficiently stressed—we must foster the desire to enter the field of education. We lack teachers! Indeed, a teacher worthy of the name can work wonders, for over and above the influence he is able to exercise directly on his students, he also has it in his power to influence the parents—a fact of the utmost significance.

BETWEEN SEMESTERS

It is vital that students of the yeshiva returning home for the vacation have a Torah *shiur* available to them, in a communal venue, e.g., a *beit medrash*, or a *shul*. Whenever school is out and the student is denied the structured activity that it alone provides, the influences that he has absorbed in the yeshivah begin to dissipate. Furthermore, when the students do in fact learn in a communal setting, and are seen at their studies by ordinary members of the community, the latter will not be indifferent to the sight and may well be moved to put in some study time of their own, or even—it's not inconceivable—to send their own children to yeshivah.

TORAH CONVENTIONS

During the vacation, something resembling a Torah convention could be organized, which hopefully would become a magnet for students from other *yeshivot*. The reverse is also desirable—our students should participate in conventions organized by students of other institutions.

PREPARING FOR THE VACATION

Before vacations it is essential to review *Hilchot Talmud Torah* with the students, for these *halachot* must verily be engraved upon their hearts. The student has to realize that the obligation of Torah study, being a *chovat gavra*, cannot be fulfilled by proxy. It is an obligation incumbent upon every Jew, young and old, not excepting the sick or the afflicted.

Even in the midst of preparations for Passover or for a family celebration, this obligation is not suspended; indeed, as soon there is a spare moment it comes immediately back into force.

We must ever be mindful of the fact that Torah study is an obligation equal in weight to all others, and an obligation that never ceases.

ELUL

With the arrival of *Elul*, an announcement would automatically go up on the wall of the yeshiva at "770": a directive from the Rebbe to the students, requiring them, during the months of *Elul* and *Tishrei*, to study chasidic *ma'amarim* whose theme is *teshuvah* and *avodah*, such as the *Igeret HaTeshuvah*, *maamarim* of *Elul* and *Rosh Chodesh*, found in *Likkutei Torah*, *Derech Chaim*, *Sha'arei Teshuvah*, *Pokei'ach Ivrim*, and so on and so forth. It is high time to reinstate this practice.

Similarly, *seforim* devoted to the topic of *teshuvah*, such as *Shaarei Teshuvah* of Rabbenu Yona, should be studied.

THE STUDENT IS THE MAIN THING

There was a time when a Rosh Yeshivah had no difficulty understanding that the students do not exist for the sake of their Rosh Yeshivah, (in order to assure him a position and a livelihood, an audience for his lectures and grist for the mill of his reputation), but the exact opposite—the Rosh Yeshivah exists for the sake of the students. Similarly, the yeshivah exists for the good of the students, and they in turn are dependent upon the Rosh Yeshivah, the *mashgiach*, and so on. The essence is, has been, and will remain: whatever serves to promote the welfare and the good of the students.

EDUCATION OF THE INNER SELF

The Rebbe, Rabbi Yosef Yitzchak, in one of his letters, (*Igrot Kodesh*, Vol. I, p. 4), directs our attention to students who are celebrated both for their Torah learning and for the wealth, and scope, of their secular knowledge. And yet, the Torah has not produced purity and refinement in their *middot*. As a result, the fear of Heaven is not their most striking characteristic. For this he holds the administrators, or *madrich*, accountable, in that, apparently, neither of them has provided the students with the proper guidance.

LETTER OF GUIDANCE

There is a letter from the Rebbe, Rabbi Yosef Yitzchak, to Rabbi Shlomo Zalman Havlin—the *mashpiah* who established Yeshivat Torat Emet in Chevron (in 5672/1912)—in which there are a number of directives relating to the guidance of the students. This letter (printed in *Igrot Kodesh*, Vol. I, p. 57) should be studied.

SHAAR HABECHINA

Every *mashpiah* should make a point of studying in private the *Shaar Ha-bechina* of *Chovat Halevovot* and mastering its contents. He will be greatly helped in his work if he does so.

CHAPTER 29
REGISTRATION

SAVING A LIFE

If we are informed that a Jewish child is in mortal danger, we are duty-bound to try and save it—failure to do so, G-d forbid, is a transgression of the commandment: "Do not stand idly by when your neighbor is in mortal danger," (*Kedoshim*, 19:16). Now if the Torah makes salvation of the body such a sacred obligation, can salvation of the soul be of a lower order! Are we not taught that one who leads another to sin is guilty of a greater wrong than one who takes his life? (*Bamidbar Rabba*, 21:5). If this is the case, even more than what threatens flesh and blood, must we fear what threatens the soul.

The saving of a Jewish soul brings with it infinite responsibilities—and a level of merit and reward commensurate with such a deed. On the other hand, one should never think one's efforts are wasted, G-d forbid, for to save even one Jewish soul is to save an entire world.

SALVATION IN PERPETUITY

The drive to increase enrollment calls for our best efforts, for when we save one child, we save not it alone, but untold generations to come.

SPREADING YIDDISHKEIT

Those of our activists who attempt to drum up enrollment in different neighborhoods must consider how to strengthen and spread Yiddishkeit on their own "turf." Apart from its inherent value in contributing to the dissemination of Judaism, this work *also* helps to swell enrollment, for such activism cleanses and purifies the atmosphere of the neighborhood, and atmosphere is a formative influence, as explained in *Hayom Yom*, (4 *Cheshvan*). An especial effort should be made to win the parents over to Yiddishkeit, something which may help them realize that they have a duty to register their children for the education that we, uniquely, can provide.

CO-OPTING YESHIVAH STUDENTS

As to whether yeshiva students may be co-opted to help with enrollment drives—the yeshivah administration should ask a *rav* if it is halachically permitted for them to take time away from their studies for this purpose.

CHAPTER 30
ADULTS/GRADUATES

A SPIRITUAL BOND

The record shows that attendance at any of the institutions founded by our *Rebbeim* has a profound influence upon the pupils who pass through them, and even when it is time to receive their certificates and go out into the world, the spiritual bond remains.

The Almighty seeks out his children when they stray, and every teacher and administrator must similarly seek out those who have now left our institutions and renew contact with them. The student should leave the school secure in the knowledge that he has a place in someone's thoughts, someone that will follow his progress with a genuine and loving concern.

Since he who teaches Torah to his neighbor's son is considered as if he himself begot him, we must ask, how *could* he banish him from his thoughts, as if he has ceased to exist? In the words of the prophet, (*Yeshayahu*, 49:15): "Can a woman forget her sucking child, that she should not have compassion on the son of her womb?" (This verse appears also in the *haftorah* of *Shabbat Parshat Eikev*, "*Vatomar Tzion*". This *haftorah* should be studied and its meaning reflected upon).

I too was a teacher, in Riga, before the Second World War. After the war I went to great lengths to track down my former students, and vowed never again to lose touch with them. Afterwards, I developed a rapport with their children, and even with their grandchildren. I can testify from my own experience that this bore an abundant harvest, in the form of the strengthening of Yiddishkeit.

CHAPTER 31
MISCELLANEOUS

DEVELOPING APTITUDES

If a student appears to have the knack or talent for a particular pursuit—we should take a positive interest and do what we can to provide the student with the opportunity to develop this ability and put it to creative use.

For example, a student with an artistic bent,—why not let her develop her talents, as long as this does not run counter to Torah values? Let her be escorted to a field, where she will be surrounded by the majesty of the Creator—"How abundant are Your works, oh L-rd, how great Your handiwork!"—and let her recreate the scene on canvas.

Similarly, if we have on our hands a student who clearly lacks the ability to learn or immerse himself in his studies, we must find ways to tap whatever other aptitudes he may have.

Take the case of the youngster who decorated his room with a beautiful wooden *aron*—ark—and other eye-pleasing features. How much satisfaction he must have had from beautifying his miniature "Beis Chabad" in this way! This will bring him to a higher level of *yirat shamayim*, love of holiness and thirst for *mitzvot*. His fellow-students will also come to appreciate the truth of the dictum: "Do not despise any man (...for there is no man who does not have his hour)," (*Avot*, 4:3), seeing that every student has his or her forte, some activity at which they excel.

BAR MITZVAH

When a boy is *bar mitzvah*, he undergoes a complete change and becomes a new entity: one who performs the commandments out of obligation, (since prior to this the voluntary element was predominant). In the eyes of the Torah he is now a rational being; accountable for his actions and punishable for his wrongdoing; whose word is believed in matters slight or serious and whose testimony is absolutely valid, even in capital cases where the court may impose the death sentence. For all intents and purposes he is an adult, with all the responsibilities of an adult.

It is up to the young man to recognize this change and make the appropriate adjustments. What he was, he was; he is now no longer the same person.

The implication of this change needs to be thoroughly understood by everyone involved with students of this age. Indeed, for a teacher recalling the young man as he was, and before this momentous change took place, this can be something of a challenge. He may find it difficult to free himself of the image of the child this young man was but a short while ago, with all the traits and failings natural to a child. As he comes, however, to appreciate this transformation more and more, it will dawn on him that now, truly, the boy is accountable for his actions. When he succeeds in sharing this insight with the student, the student in turn will be helped to view the revolution that has overtaken him with a little more detachment, and enabled to assume his new status with less awkwardness, as his conduct will no doubt quickly demonstrate.

SUPPLEMENTARY LEARNING

The Rebbe has called for an increase in Torah learning. In response, I propose that, on a daily basis, every class, continue an additional five minutes into one of the regular breaks, and that the students have the arrangement explained to them in these terms. This should apply across the board, to everyone and to every class.

A SPECIFIC PROPOSAL

As is known, every *Rosh HaShana* we take upon ourselves an additional *hiddur*—seeking to perform a particular mitzvah to the best of our capacities. In light of this, I have a proposal for the coming year.

Positive mitzvah—*Shabbat* observance.

Negative mitzvah—Controlling one's thoughts.

Good *middah*—Cultivating a good heart.

Speak at length on these matters and motivate the students to be mindful of them and act upon them in the best possible way. Similarly, working with the students on illustrative projects will help get the lesson across.

MEN TEACHING GIRLS

It is not fitting for men to teach girls and women to teach boys, as this can lead to a variety of problems that are best avoided in the first place.

A NEGATIVE INFLUENCE

What of the student who comes into the classroom and treats his friends to a vivid account of what he saw on television the night before? The answer is that we must take him aside and explain to him that few transgressions can rival in gravity the case of the sinner who leads others to sin. The teacher should take him through the passages in *Hilchot Teshuvah* of the Rambam, (chap. 4, *halacha* 1), dealing with a person who causes others to transgress. Because of the enormity of this sin, such a person is not given the opportunity to repent, and it is almost beyond human means to repair the damage caused.

Approaching the matter from a different angle, we should also explain to him what is meant by, "Who is a hero? One who conquers his evil impulse." Reflecting on this he might be persuaded to stop from sharing these experiences with his friends. As a result, he might, further down the road, decide to give up television himself. Indeed, he might even encourage others to do so. We must make him understand, though, that his obligation extends even to working to undo the bad influence that he has already had on his friends, with all its possible consequences.

SEPARATING BETWEEN HOLY AND PROFANE

The policy in Lubavitch is for secular studies to be taught in the afternoon only. If there is no alternative, they may take place in the morning, but the day must commence with religious studies.

There are institutions in which religious and secular are mixed together, one hour of this and one hour of that, without distinction. Every effort must be made to avoid such an arrangement.

TEXTS FOR SECULAR SUBJECTS

Textbooks in secular subjects must not violate the spirit of Judaism, which is one of holiness and purity. If the book contains heretical material, (such as the supposed age of the world), or immorality—it is not to be used. The same goes for a book in which the illustrative material serves no educational purpose.

Exactly the same concern applies to textbooks on math, history, science, social studies, and so on.

THE SCREENING OF FILMS

Generally, what we see leaves a much deeper impression upon us than what we hear. Something seen buries itself deep within the psyche and can be recalled even decades later.

It is not necessary, therefore, to emphasize how important it is to protect our students from films that encourage those watching them to identify with the actors and to copy their behavior—such as going bare-headed, without *tzitzit*, not to mention acts of violence, murder, and so on. The student dwells on these spectacles and they return to populate his dreams.

We must then be careful to check every film before it is shown to the students. We are not advocating a wholesale ban on the screening of films, but the films obtained should be educational and positive in outlook and should serve to impart knowledge, even when they are humorous and entertaining.

THE MAXIMUM OF EDUCATION

Ahavat Yisrael obliges us to secure for the young the maximum in education and the soundest values. Just as we can never have enough nutrients stored in our bodies but are constantly trying to supplement them, so it is with *chinuch*. If we content ourselves with only a minimum of it, it's to be feared that even the paltry amount the child does receive may do him more harm than good.

HOLY SHEEP

Jewish children are called "Holy Sheep." It is the nature of sheep to cry *"Meh! Meh!"* The child asks *"Meh?"*—in Hebrew, "What?"—and we must answer him. . . .

GOOD WISHES, NOTHING MORE

When a male child is born or has reached bar-mitzvah, it is customary to extend good wishes to the parents: *may the boy grow up to be a* chassid, *a G-d-fearing man and a scholar!* But—do we really know what we are saying? And what do we parents and teachers actually do to make these wishes a reality? It all comes down to little more than banalities—banalities and pious sentiments. . . .

EDUCATIONAL TOYS

Education in the truest sense begins at the moment of birth, and especially when the child begins to show signs of understanding, at age one or one and a half. The child is developing rapidly during this period, and we must fill its waking hours with games and pastimes that have genuinely educational content. Unfortunately, most mothers have not learned how to use their child's playtime to the best educational advantage since, understandably, they are anxious to avoid too much disruption of their household routine.

Similarly, even when the child begins daycare or playgroup, on its return home the mother should fill the hours before bedtime with some sort of positive activity. The problem is, however, that she knows not what nor how—and the problem only becomes more insistent during vacation time, *Shabbat* and festivals.

An idea worth trying is to form a committee of kindergarten workers who themselves are mothers—women of experience in early childhood education and the home—whose mission will be to mull over the problem and put forward a variety of proposals. These would then be circulated in a special publication dedicated to this topic.

After their researches are concluded, they may well, with persistence, succeed in persuading some manufacturers of toys and games to create and market a line of toys designed to meet the educational needs that they have identified.

LEARNING *ALEPH-BEIT*

. . . There is a spiritual component to our method of teaching *Aleph Beit*, which is designed to provide a solid foundation for the education of the child. Additionally, this method has important pedagogic advantages.

It goes without saying that like any system this requires the know-how capable of making it into an effective educational tool—something difficult to elaborate upon in a letter.

At any event, when we discuss this method with teachers, it is most important to help and assist them in its use, to enable them to exploit it to the maximum. This method of teaching *Aleph Beit* must not be abandoned, come what may—it is too awesome a responsibility.

ON THE DRAFTING OF A GUIDE TO READING

a) When studying the *Aleph-Beit*, the child's eye should at the very outset light upon the true form of the letters, not an approximation of it. Otherwise, he might be led to imagine that the inferior version represents the actual form of the letter, which of course is not the case.

b) The order in which the *nekudot* are learned should follow our time-honored practices, as in the *Aleph Beit* Chart (printed as a separate item, both in the *siddur* and the text-books). Over and above the fact that this particular arrangement has its foundation in the holy sources, it also makes excellent sense to avoid confusion in the way the learning of this is structured, given the fact that parts of the *Aleph-Beit* are sometimes divided up between parents and various teachers.

(It is particularly important that they begin with *kamats*, and not with *patach*, since from their earliest years they have been used to hearing the *Aleph-Beit* learned in the sequence: *kamats-aleph-ah*.

c) It is advisable to refer to the book, *Mavo Lekri'ah*, published by Merkos L'Inyonei Chinuch. An answer will be found there to the question concerning the combination of *nekudot* as applied to the learning of the other letters.

CHAPTER 32
PARENTAL DUTY

A LIVING EXAMPLE

Parents must never lose sight of the fact that—from a child's earliest age—their own behavior, even in the world beyond the home, is a major determinant in the formation of its character—and to a much greater extent than they might think possible. A crucial part of the child's education depends upon the sights and sounds to which it is exposed at home, in the milieu created by its parents.

A boy who regards his father as the living embodiment of certain qualities, will want to be like him, will respect him and will conduct himself towards him in the proper way.

Incidentally, a great deal of this depends upon the mother, for the child's education is, more than not, left to her discretion.

When the father makes the wisest use of his time, participates in *shiurim* and studies actively; *davens* regularly three times a day with a *minyan*; does not talk during *davening*; and so on—his example is absorbed by the child and becomes the blueprint for his own behavior.

It is futile to expect a child to have set times for Torah study when this is not the custom in his own home, (and a father simply cannot demand of his son something that he finds too bothersome to do himself). In the child's mind Torah learning will be lumped together with other kinds of schoolwork, and he will look forward to the day when he is "exempt" from it all—just like his father.

THE ATMOSPHERE OF THE HOME

Parents must not fall into the error of thinking that the atmosphere in the home will not have a truly telling effect upon their children's development. They must always keep in mind that for a full and rounded education a positive atmosphere is a must, in the home every bit as much as in the school. We do everything in our power to keep a child away from street corners, fearing that he or she will be influenced by the coarse atmosphere of such places, and become inured to it. In the same way, we must strive to bring the atmosphere of the home into harmony with that of the school, and prevent it from undermining what the school is trying to achieve.

We have witnessed of late a universal outcry regarding pollution of the air and the degrading of the environment. Certainly it is true that a pure and pristine atmosphere contributes its share to the totality of a person, his psychology, the quality of his learning and his character traits, (see Rashi, *Sh'lach*, 13:18). The same applies in the spiritual realm—the success of education depends to a very great extent on the spiritual atmosphere that surrounds the child. When parents come to appreciate what a formidable influence the home, and the atmosphere of the home, have on the education of their children, and decide to act on this knowledge, they will also discover how substantial a contribution, direct and indirect, they themselves can make to its success.

THE MERITS OF THE FATHERS

There are those who take justifiable pride in their father or grandfather, and turn the merit of this *yichus* to their advantage. Parents should be concerned that their offspring, will be able to bask in the merit of *their* parents and grandparents, and this— through their own efforts to live up to the highest standards, to be *"sheine elteren"*—model parents.

The parents who truly desire the best for their children, (and is there any other kind!), have it in their power to make them a gift. This gift possesses three unique properties: all the money in the world cannot buy it; the child can receive it only from its parents; and, the child can acquire it by absolutely no other means. What is this gift?—The fact that he or she has *"sheine elteren!"* . . . . model parents.

DAVENING WITH A MINYAN

The obligation to *daven* with a *minyan* is second to none. Parents *must* take their children to the synagogue to pray with a *minyan!*

The above applies to younger siblings too, and not only to children who are already well used to praying. They must be brought to the *shul* in order to answer *Amen* and *y'hei sh'mey rabbah*, until they come to feel that they are in their element.

Naturally, it sends a powerful message to the child when the father himself behaves like a *mentsch* in the synagogue.

HILCHOT CHINUCH

It is the duty of the parents to study and know the *halachot* pertinent to *chinuch*, for the education of the child is committed to their hands no less than to the teacher's.

MAINTAINING RESPECT FOR THE EDUCATOR

Parents are forbidden to speak disparagingly of a teacher in front of their child, even if they consider such behavior justified. When the teacher's character or conduct is so unambiguously called into question, the first to suffer will be the child himself, who will no longer be able to benefit from the teacher's instruction and may well be left in a state of spiritual impoverishment. It may turn out that at a later date the teacher is able to vindicate himself, or clear his name, but the child is now removed from the scene, and there is no undoing the damage that has been done. These are the hard facts.

SHOPPING DURING SCHOOL HOURS

A serious breakdown of standards in certain schools is taking place before our eyes. The administrators are standing by and watching while parents spirit their children out of the classroom and send them shopping, or on other errands. We must put a stop to this abuse once and for all. Word must go out that the education of our children cannot be sacrificed for anything—not even the building of the *Beit Hamikdash*, (*Shabbat*, 119b)—how much more so to things of infinitely less importance.

CHAPTER 33
THE PARENT AND THE SCHOOL

EDUCATING THE PARENTS

The education of the student takes place both in the school and in the home. In certain circumstances, the school must educate the parents, too.

STAYING IN TOUCH

The connection with the parents must be made as early as first grade, not delayed until grades five or six.

COOPERATION

The whole question of cooperation with parents and the legitimate interest that we take in having the atmosphere in the home complement and strengthen the atmosphere of the school itself— in my view, none of this is taken seriously enough. We must remedy the situation, therefore, by making the appropriate change in priorities.

We should hold educational conferences from time to time, with a view to examining this sort of cooperation, formulating proposals and initiating programs designed to augment it.

THE ACTIONS OF THE FATHERS—
A HAPPY PORTENT FOR THE CHILDREN

A letter should be circulated among the parents, in which we stress our shared responsibility for the education of their children. We must direct their attention to the fact that the student spends only a part of his or her day in the school, and is also exposed to the influence of the street and the home, especially during vacations. Of course, the parents have their own lives to lead, but, in the final analysis, all depends upon the care and thought that they devote to this question.

We must explain to them that, beside the direct influences on their children, there are more subtle ones as well. A case in point: the child understands the extent to which his father does or does not maintain a learning schedule, *davens* with a *minyan*, etc. Also to be reckoned with is the impact of the domestic scene—the atmosphere in the home, relationships with neighbors, the company the parents keep.

It is also vital to explain how great an impact the parents' *middot* can have on their children. When, for example, the father cannot talk to his son without shouting at him, the son will most likely inherit the same negative trait; whereas, when he is spoken to with a modicum of civility, the son will surely want to mirror this in his own behavior.

One letter should be sent before the summer, an additional one at the beginning of the new year.

THE PROPER WAY TO RELATE

When parents call upon the principal of the school or his assistants, to make inquiries or to air their grievances, they should be met with patience and courtesy. In a word, they should be made to feel welcome, not, G-d forbid, treated in a high-handed manner. When the school behaves ineptly on such occasions, the parents are left with the damaging impression that no one attaches any importance to what they think or feel.

A point to consider—in olden times the teacher was paid directly by the parents, when, curiously enough, he had no problem at all showing his employer the proper respect. All this has changed, though not necessarily for the better.

A flawed relationship with the parents of any child is likely to have far-reaching consequences. If they leave the premises smarting with the indignities that have been heaped upon them, they will lose no time picking the teacher and the school apart, painting them in the blackest colors and finding fault with everything, (all this on account of their miserable reception). At the same time their child will be taking in every word, the end result being that such respect and affection as he may have felt towards the teacher is now permanently soured.

And the long-term effect?—A breakdown in discipline, and the loss of the rapport that existed between teacher and child, bringing with it unfortunate consequences for both. Predictably, there will be a decline in the child's behavior and academic standards. This in turn will be used to justify the parents' decision to remove him from the school and enroll him elsewhere, (oftentimes—a much-inferior choice given the level of *yirat shamayim* he is likely to meet with). Worst of all, the parents will malign the school in front of their neighbors and acquaintances, even influencing other parents, on the impulse of the moment, to cancel any plans they may have had to enroll their children there.

What begins, then, as a relatively minor incident—parents dealt with in an offhand manner and smarting at their treatment—leads step by step to this disastrous conclusion. Isn't it generally the case that we all wish the Almighty to be content with us? And isn't the way to achieve this—that, first, our *fellow man* should be content with us, as the *Mishnah* itself declares? (*Avot*, 3:10).

THE HEART OF THE FATHER IS WON OVER BY THE SON

A teacher who has in his class a student whose parents are opposed to the level of *yirat shamayim* in the school, has a duty to look for ways to win them over. By the same token, the student needs to be treated in such a way that, in the end, roles are reversed, as it were, and it is he who lovingly influences his parents for the good.

ASSEMBLIES BEFORE THE PARENT BODY

When parents attend school events, we should try to persuade one of the parents to give a *d'var Torah*, and follow this with one from a student representing the school. This should help bring home to the parents that Torah learning is not just the preserve of *rabbonim* and of those who sit in *yeshivah* all day, but that the Torah is the inheritance and entitlement of the entire community, parents and students, layman and professional, alike.

Food and drink should be laid on for the guests, and parents and students can make the appropriate blessings. This will be useful both for the parents, (who may have a yen to repeat it when they get home), and for the students, (who will see that "father is also making a blessing").

Every assembly should include a segment on the Ten Mitzvah Campaigns initiated by the Rebbe.

TORAH CLASSES FOR THE MOTHERS OF THE STUDENTS

How satisfying it would be to see Torah classes being organized for the mothers of the students, a few times a week. In a number of the schools there are vacant classrooms, and the *shiur* could be held in one of them. Similarly, it should be possible to arrange child-care while mothers are attending the class.

ADDITIONS

ADDITION A:

Free translation of the section beginning: "Usefartem Lachem," Sefer Maamarim in Yiddish, p. 115 (pertaining to chap. 27)

Explanation of the seven *middot* contained within the *middah* of *chesed* as they exist in the faculties of the *nefesh* and the *middot* of the heart.

Chesed—its character is love. This love brings about the act of kindness, as stated in the verse: (*Yirmiyah*, 31:2), "I have loved you with an eternal love, therefore have I showered you with kindness, (*chesed*)."

Chesed within *chesed*—revealed love, the welling up of an inner and instinctive love, like the love of a father for his child. Although the love of the father is instinctive, unconditional and not affected in any way by its revelation, nevertheless, when it is revealed and evident to all, it is *chesed* within *chesed*.

G'vurah, or severity, within *chesed* arises when the attribute of *chesed* clothes itself within another attribute which is its total antithesis. *Chesed* is love and *gevurah* is enmity. *Gevurah* within *chesed* is the enmity which is born of *chesed*—hence, one's feelings of hostility towards the enemy of his friend.

Tiferet within *chesed*—*Tiferet* is spiritual beauty and/or mercy. For example, a picture painted in a variety of hues will be lovelier than one done only in black. *Tiferet* is, accordingly, a blend of *chesed* and *gevurah*, enabling us to deal, say, with an individual who is not deserving of *chesed*, but with whom one is reluctant—out of feelings of mercy—to treat too harshly (*gevurah*), although such treatment is warranted. *Tiferet* within *chesed* is the beauty of *chesed*, that is, employing *chesed* only for spiritually fruitful ends, such as *tzedakah*, the spreading of Torah knowledge, and the like, for "those who practice this, it (*tiferet*) garbs with splendor."

Netzach within *chesed* is the attribute of acting toward another with the proper degree of *chesed*, under any and all circumstances, and allowing nothing to deflect him from his course.

Hod within *chesed* is the expression of that love symbolized by the readiness to sacrifice his life in place of his friend's.

Y'sod within *chesed* is the mighty bond of love connecting the one who loves, to the beloved.

Malchut within *chesed* finds expression in words of love and affection addressed to the beloved.

Thus far we have dealt with human character traits. Man's possession of intellect and emotion is what sets him off from the animal world. While animals also possess intelligence and emotion, these differ radically from man's in two critical respects: a) Man is distinguished primarily by his intellect, and this faculty governs his emotions; the animal world is driven by emotion, to which its intelligence is forever in thrall. b) The emotional and intelligential features of animal life never rise above the level of instinct. The Jew, by contrast, differs from the rest of humanity, in that his intellectual and emotional powers originate, beyond their foundation in the rational, with actual G-dliness. G-dly intellect and emotion embody a spiritual force that enables them—acting through the rational intellect and emotion—to affect man's intellect and emotion even when they function on the instinctive level. The constituent parts of this instinctive intellect and emotion are the animal soul and the *yetzer hara*: the former corresponding to intellect, the latter to emotion.

The Seven *middot* of the animal soul and *yetzer hara:*

Chesed—the love for the things of the world, of the life of the flesh.

Chesed within *chesed* is the intoxicated involvement a person may have—Heaven forfend—with earthly delights and worldly doctrines of every kind.

G'vurah within *chesed*—is the intestinal hatred felt towards the Jew who observes Torah and *mitzvot.*

Tiferet within *chesed* may be discerned in one to whom the words of the Psalmist (*Tehillim*, 10:3), apply: "For the wicked man exults over the lusts of his soul."

Netzach within *chesed*—expresses itself in the determination, not only to wallow in sin himself, but in doing his level best to get others to wallow in it with him.

Hod within *chesed*—one who possesses this attribute "knows his Creator and desires to rebel against Him." He sins and abandons the path of righteousness, not so much out of pleasure and desire, or because he cannot help himself, as out of a spirit of malicious defiance, of spite towards his Maker.

Yesod within *chesed*—one who possesses this attributes lives for the gratification of his senses. Indeed, he will kill for their sake, and for their sake no risk is too great, even if it leads to the ruination of his health and to pay for it with his life.

Malchut within *chesed* refers to the unchecked growth of prohibited speech in general, and of atheism in particular: entailing the denial of G-d and His Torah, behavior typical of those who deny G-d and scoff at his *mitzvot*—both in word and in print. [The reckless and irresponsible conduct of freethinker and heretic coarsens the world and stands in brute contradiction to the purpose G-d intended for His Creation, namely, that Jews through Torah-study and performance of *mitzvot* refine and elevate the world.

Jews refine and elevate the world by utilizing the G-dly intellectual and emotional traits of their divine soul. *[Chesed,* and the seven emotional attributes within *chesed* of the G-dly soul are:]

Chesed—the natural and instinctive love of the G-dly soul for G-d.

Chesed within *chesed*—the revelation of this natural love to the point where it pervades all the faculties, and is not limited to the heart alone. Herein lies the distinction between loving G-d "with all your heart" and loving Him "with all your soul." "With all your soul" extends to all the faculties and powers of the individual, raising him above the life of the senses, beyond the reach of the world's idea.

Gevurah within *chesed*—hatred towards those who hate G-d, as in, (*Tehillim*, 97:10), "Those who love G-d hate evil," as is said, (*Tehillim*, 139:22), "with an ultimate hatred do I hate them."

Tiferet within *chesed*—the channeling of the creative powers and inclinations of the soul into (the beautification of) Torah and *mitzvot*, [as the verse states:] "And his heart was lifted up in the ways of the L-rd."

Netzach within *chesed*—the triumph in the contest with the animal soul and the *yetzer hara*, which lie vanquished at his feet.

Hod within *chesed*—he pits himself with the utmost ferocity against the scoffers and the apostates, denouncing them, and negating their influence on the Jewish people.

Yesod within *chesed*—binding oneself to Torah and *mitzvot* in a spirit of total self-sacrifice.

Malchut within *chesed*—one's lips never cease from uttering words of Torah and prayer.